STUDENT
Cook Book

SILVANA FRANCO

D0994393

MEREHURST

Published in 1995 by Merehurst Limited
Ferry House, 51–57 Lacy Road, Putney, London SW15 1PR

Reprinted 1995, 1996

Copyright © 1995 Merehurst Limited

ISBN 1–85391–426–6

A catalogue record for this book is available from the British Library

Series Editor: Valerie Barrett
Design: Clive Dorman
Illustrations: Keith Sparrow

Typeset by Clive Dorman & Co.
Colour Separation by P&W Graphics Pty Ltd, Singapore
Printed and bound in Great Britain by
Mackays of Chatham PLC, Chatham, Kent

RECIPE NOTES

 Indicates dishes that cook in under 35 minutes

- Follow one set of measurements only, do not mix metric and imperial
- All spoon measures are level
- Always taste and adjust seasonings to suit your own preferences

V Indicates dishes that are suitable for vegetarians

CONTENTS

INTRODUCTION

Becoming a student usually means leaving home, and for the first time being completely responsible for your own money, cleaning, washing and of course, cooking. Bearing in mind that time and money are of the essence, you may think that bothering to cook for yourself is a waste of precious time and energy that could be better spent studying or drinking in the pub. But there are a few very good reasons why you should take the time to cook and eat properly.

You need a balanced, healthy diet to function to the best of your ability both physically and mentally. Cooking your own food from scratch is cheaper and healthier than ready-made meals and take-away food. It's also great fun. Invite friends for a meal and impress them with your inventiveness and creativity, and don't forget, if you're living in a shared house full of students, as the cook, you get to skip the washing up.

This is a basic book, with dishes that you will be able to master even if you've never boiled an egg before. All the recipes are very straightforward, giving plenty of scope for you to adapt them and make them your own. Save time in the kitchen by being well prepared and planning what you're going to cook in advance. If your cupboard is well stocked, you should be able to knock up a meal for two without having to go out for extra ingredients. Most of the recipes in this book serve two. If you're only cooking for yourself, it's still worth making the full quantity and then reheating it the next day or taking it to college with you for your lunch.

A good time-saving way to balance your meals is to cook all-in-one complete meals based on a carbohydrate such as pasta or rice and to help you stick to these guidelines, this book includes chapters based upon the four main carbohydrates. If you make dishes that need an accompaniment, steam some fresh vegetables or make a quick salad rather than choosing chips. See page 6 for nutritional information which includes more details on meal planning. Happy cooking!!

EATING WELL

Eating well is the key to getting the best from life. If you plan to cram your revision or study late into the night, it is essential that you eat a well-balanced diet that will not only keep your mind and body fuelled, but can also help prevent heart disease, tooth decay and obesity as well as many other common illnesses. Studies have shown, for example, that you're less likely to get a cold if you have a good intake of vitamin C, which is something to think about if you've got exams looming.

Generally speaking, the more varied your diet, the more likely it is that all the vital nutrients you need are being provided. In order to ensure you are getting enough you must be eating from each of the three main food groups detailed below. Having discovered how to plan good balanced meals, you should also take a look at the snacks you eat between meals. Try to drink plenty of water and eat yogurts or fruit if you get hunger pangs – sugary drinks and fried salty snacks will just help you to pile on the pounds, and offer very little by way of nutrients.

GROUP 1:

CARBOHYDRATES

Starchy foods like potatoes and bread are good sources of fibre, vitamins and minerals. Carbohydrates like these should be the base of every meal, they are naturally low in fat (and as a nation, we consume far more fat than we need), and will satisfy your hunger.

Your body needs carbohydrates to convert into energy but there are two main types: starch and sugar. When you eat a sugar-filled food or drink, you get an almost instant energy surge, which is quickly followed by a low. Your brain tells you that you need more energy and you crave for another bar of chocolate or can of fizzy pop. Yo-yoing energy levels can leave you feeling lethargic and unable to concentrate on your studies. Because starches are digested by the body far more slowly than sugars, they give a constant slow-releasing source of energy which is exactly what you need if you're going into a three-hour exam. If you have a heavy day ahead, you must eat a proper breakfast. When you wake up, your sugar levels are low so boost them up with sustaining food. Have a couple of slices of toast and Marmite and a big bowl of muesli or porridge, avoid tea or coffee and have a glass of fresh orange juice instead.

At meal times go for filled baked potatoes, risottos and stews and pair stir-fries, soups or salads with a carbohydrate for a healthy, well-balanced meal. Good carbohydrates include:

rice and grains

pulses:	lentils, beans and dried peas
breakfast cereals:	muesli, porridge and Shredded Wheat, not sugar coated Frosties or Ricicles
bread:	wholemeal is best but white is still good

pasta

potatoes

noodles

GROUP 2

PROTEIN

The body needs protein for the production of body tissue, so to keep strong and healthy it must be included in your diet. Most people in this country easily consume enough protein so it is not something that you really need to worry about, but it is worth keeping an eye on if you are vegetarian, constantly dieting, or on a very limited budget for food. You don't need to consume a lot but should make an effort to include a small amount with each meal. Unfortunately a lot of high protein food is also high fat, so choose lean meat and trim off any fat, and be aware of how much cheese, cream and butter you eat.

The type and quality of protein varies greatly in different foods. Animal proteins such as fish, milk and poultry are the most complete, but there are plenty of good, but not quite as complex plant sources of protein to be found in carbohydrates like grains, pulses, beans and potatoes. The best way to ensure quality, not just quantity is to try and combine proteins so they complement each other. This is particularly important if you're vegetarian and even more so for vegans who don't eat dairy produce. Try and eat at least two different foods together to obtain a high quality protein, fortunately this is the way that most foods go together anyway – a good example is beans on toast which is a very good high fibre, high protein, low-fat snack meal. Quality high protein foods include:

fish and shell fish	**lean meat**
poultry	**milk**
yogurt	**cheese**
eggs	**butter**
tofu	**nuts**
seeds	**peanut butter**

GROUP 3

EATING WELL

FRUIT & VEGETABLES

The World Health Organisation recommends that we eat at least 400g, that's almost a pound, or five portions of fruit and vegetables a day – that doesn't include potatoes but does include beans, nuts and seeds. Fruit and vegetables are packed with different vitamins and minerals, so you should try and vary the types you eat and remember that it's impossible to eat too much. Choose fresh or dried fruit in preference to a bar of chocolate or crisps.

The way that you cook the vegetables is of the utmost importance, as it is very easy to destroy the nutrients. Leafy greens are packed with water-soluble vitamin C, so the traditional method of boiling them in water means that when you eat the vegetables, you may still get the fibre but the nutrients and most of the flavour have gone down the drain. Instead try stir-frying, steaming or cooking methods which involve eating the liquid that the vegetables have been cooked in such as soups, stews and pasta sauces.

As soon as they are harvested, fruit and green vegetables begin to deteriorate nutritionally. Don't store them for weeks but eat within a few days of buying. Frozen and canned vegetables are just as good, and in some cases better than fresh. Take frozen spinach for example, which is picked, prepared and quickly frozen within hours, locking in a good percentage of the nutrients

SUMMARY

- Base your meals on starchy carbohydrates to get a constant supply of energy

- Cut back on sugary snacks – don't satisfy your hunger with empty calories that leave you craving more.

- Try to avoid stimulants such as chocolate, cola and coffee – keep your mind and body on an even keel.

- Ensure you get enough high quality protein – try and eat at least 2 together

- Keep an eye on your fat intake, including butter, cream and cheese

- Try to eat five portions of fruit and vegetables each day – take care when preparing and cooking vegetables, don't destroy their vitamin content.

FOOD SAFETY

The most important thing to remember when you're responsible for feeding yourself, is to keep the kitchen clean. It isn't all that difficult to give yourself (or your house-mates) food poisoning, but if you cook your food carefully and observe basic hygiene and storage rules, you won't put anybody's health at risk.

Here are a few pointers that you should keep in mind:

- Keep the kitchen floor clean, don't encourage mice, rats and other vermin to set up home in your house.

- Don't let dirty pots pile up or bacteria will multiply at an astonishing rate, making your kitchen unsafe and smelly. While you're cooking, try and wash-up as you go and finish off washing the rest straight after you've eaten.

- Wash up in very hot , soapy water. Use rubber gloves and a scrubbing brush and take care to rinse the dishes well with clean hot water.

- Leave the washing-up to air-dry on the draining board – dirty tea towels will just spread germs onto a clean plate, so make sure they're laundered regularly.

- Clean up splashes and spillages immediately after they occur as they make the floor dangerously slippery and can become ingrained and harbour bacteria. Bits of food on the floor and under the cooker can also encourage the odd mouse or two to set up home in your kitchen.

- Wash your hands before you start cooking.

- Keep the fridge clean. It's easy to forget a small lump of cheese that's left to go green at the back of the fridge, if it's not cleaned out regularly. Mould quickly spreads from bad food to healthy like the one bad apple in the sack. It's not only risky but costly.

- Never keep food past its sell-by date.

- If a chilled item has been left out of the fridge and has become warm, play safe and throw it away, especially if it's made from dairy produce.

- Store raw meat properly wrapped up and well away from cooked foods. It is better to keep raw meat at the bottom of the fridge so that there's no danger of blood dripping down on to cooked food.

- Use a separate chopping board for raw meat as contamination, particularly from pork and poultry to other foods is common. Scrub boards thoroughly after use.

- Wash your hands thoroughly after touching meat. Take care not to touch pan handles, knives or tea towels whilst preparing raw meat and before you have washed your hands.

- Store dry goods in a cool dark place. Keep bags sealed up with tape and check sell-by dates.

- Take chilled or frozen food home as quickly as possible and store at the correct temperature. Don't

FOOD SAFETY

refreeze food that has defrosted.

● Take care when defrosting food especially meat, fish and poultry. Never force food to defrost quickly but leave it wrapped up at room temperature or even better, in the fridge until completely thawed. Don't ever be tempted by helpful friends who suggest 'rinsing the frozen prawns under the hot tap', or 'leaving the chicken in the sink full of hot water, or in the airing cupboard' to defrost.

● Don't reheat food more than once.

EQUIPMENT

Whether you choose to lodge in college accommodation or a shared house or flat, you'll probably have to share kitchen facilities with a group of other students. This can be a bit of a mixed bag of tricks. No doubt you will argue about whose turn it is to wash-up or empty the bin, but on the plus side, you will have the opportunity to pool resources, not just borrowing the ketchup from your house-mate's cupboard, but sharing kitchen utensils and equipment. Every High Street has a cheap kitchen shop that's an Aladdin's Cave of useful gadgets from spatulas and can openers to salad spinners and fancy vegetable slicers, so you should be able to get your hands on the essentials listed below. And don't forget that any piece of equipment you buy, is an investment that you'll probably use for years.

ESSENTIALS:

- can opener
- cheese grater
- rolling pin
- slotted spoon
- fish slice
- potato masher
- pastry brush
- 2 chopping boards (1 for raw meat)
- 3 wooden spoons
- metal hand whisk
- metal sieve
- frying pan
- 3 sizes of saucepan with lids
- 2 sizes of bowl
- 1 large sharp knife
- 1 small sharp knife
- set of kitchen scales
- baking sheet
- roasting tin
- casserole dish with lid

NOT ESSENTIAL BUT VERY HANDY

- garlic press
- vegetable peeler
- measuring jug
- wok

INGREDIENTS

If you've only got half a cupboard and a shelf in the fridge to store your provisions, then you're going to have to think carefully about what you buy, or you'll end up with a cupboard packed with pickled gherkins, 3 varieties of mango chutney, a tub of glacé cherries and no room for your bread or pasta.

Here's a list of all the things you ought to have in store. Apart from the items listed, buy vegetables and salad ingredients to accompany meals, and keep some fresh fruit handy to munch after supper or if you're feeling peckish.

CUPBOARD

INGREDIENTS

ESSENTIALS
- packet of pasta
- packet of long grain rice
- can of chopped plum tomatoes
- can of baked beans
- can of tuna
- small bottle of olive oil
- small bottle of vegetable oil
- bottle of soy sauce
- small bag of lentils
- small tub of dried parsley
- small tub of dried basil
- carton of curry powder
- packet of stock cubes
- tube of tomato purée
- bottle of vinegar
- small packet of flour
- bag of sugar
- salt and pepper

NOT ESSENTIAL, BUT VERY HANDY
- jar of English mustard
- bottle of Worcestershire sauce
- can of corned beef
- can of chickpeas
- can of anchovies in oil
- bottle of tomato ketchup
- jar of honey

- jar of pesto sauce
- cumin seeds
- dried chillies

FRIDGE

INGREDIENTS

There are very few chilled items that are real essentials, but there are some that you will use almost everyday. I have not included fresh herbs, as they are something of a luxury for most students, but why not have a go at growing your own – a small pot from the supermarket is not too pricey and with a bit of attention, will survive happily on a sunny windowsill. Alternatively, if you have freezer space, keep a packet of fresh parsley in there, and simply crumble a handful into your cooking as you need it. Other good things to keep in your fridge are a jar of mayonnaise and a jar of curry paste.

ESSENTIALS

- Milk
- Butter or Margarine
- Eggs
- Cheese (Cheddar & Parmesan). Cheese adds flavour to your cooking so it's well worth shelling out a little extra for a tangy, mature Cheddar that will really zip up your food rather than opting for the cheaper but blander, mild Cheddars. The same applies to fresh Parmesan. It is expensive, but a little of it, freshly grated, goes a long way. If you're planning to eat plenty of delicious pasta dishes, then the dried, ready-grated variety won't do your cooking any favours.

POTATOES

There are basically two types of potato, new and old. Although new potatoes are available all year, they are at their best in the spring. Small, waxy and firm they are thin skinned and should be eaten soon after buying. They taste delicious steamed, boiled or stir-fried in olive oil. Old potatoes are thicker skinned and are from the second harvest of the year, they are hardy enough to stand longer lengths of storage and are great for roasting, baking, mashing and making chips.

INTRODUCTION

Don't buy or eat potatoes that have turned green. Cut out any eyes, and sprouting, blackened or bruised areas from the potatoes before you cook them. Store them in a brown paper bag in your food cupboard or some other cool, dark, dry place.

BOILING

If using old potatoes, peel or scrub them well, cutting out all blemishes. Cut into quarters and place in a large saucepan. Cover with cold water, add a pinch of salt and bring to the boil. Simmer for about 20 minutes or so until tender. If you are boiling potatoes for mash, use old ones and cut them into small pieces to speed up cooking time. If you're boiling new potatoes, scrub them well, but don't peel. Put them into salted boiling water and cook for 10-20 minutes depending upon their size, until tender.

BAKING

See Classic Baked Potatoes on page 38.

ROASTING

Preheat the oven to 190C, 375F, Gas 5. Place 3-4 table-spoons of vegetable oil in a roasting tin and put in the oven to heat. Peel the potatoes and cut into quarters, put into the tin with a sprinkle of salt and toss well with the hot fat. Roast for about 1-1½ hours, turning occasionally until crisp on the outside and soft and fluffy on the inside. If you want to speed up cooking time, boil the potatoes for about 8 minutes before roasting. Add flavour to roast potatoes by cooking them with a couple of whole garlic cloves and a sprig of fresh herbs such as rosemary or sage.

MAKING CHIPS

The best way to cook chips is to fry them twice. If you're going to make your own chips, it's well worth the trouble of doing it properly, as it is the only way to get good crisp chips that are also soft and fluffy inside. Scrub the potatoes in clean cold water and cut into fingers as thick or thin as you like. Wash well, rinsing off excess starch to stop them sticking together, and dry thoroughly with kitchen paper. Heat a couple of inches of vegetable oil in a small deep frying pan until a cube of bread, when dropped in, turns brown in about a minute. Cook the chips for 5 minutes or until pale golden. Remove with a slotted spoon and drain on kitchen paper. Raise the heat slightly and when the oil is hot enough to brown a cube of bread in 30 seconds, return the chips to the pan for 1-2 minutes until crisp. Drain on kitchen paper and sprinkle with salt.

SAUSAGE, BAKED BEAN AND POTATO HOTPOT

REALLY EASY!

Serves 2

350g (12 oz) potatoes, peeled and halved if large
1 teaspoon vegetable oil
250g (8 oz) sausages, cut into bite-sized pieces
1 large onion, sliced
400g (14 oz) can of baked beans
knob of butter or margarine
seasoning

1 Preheat the oven to 200C,400F,Gas 6. Partially cook the potatoes in salted boiling water for 10 minutes. Drain and set aside to cool slightly.

2 Meanwhile, heat the oil in a large frying pan and cook the sausage pieces for 5 minutes until golden. Remove with a slotted spoon and set aside. Add the onion slices to the same pan and fry over a high heat for 5 minutes until tender and golden. The sausages will have released some of their fat into the pan so it shouldn't be necessary to add any extra oil.

3 Return the sausage pieces plus the baked beans to the frying pan, heat through and season to taste. Spoon the mixture into a deep casserole dish.

4 Thinly slice the potatoes and arrange them over the top of the bean mixture, overlapping them. Dot with butter, cover with a lid or foil and bake for 10 minutes. Remove covering and cook for a further 10 minutes until cooked through and golden-brown around the edges.

SPANISH TORTILLA

E A S Y !

Tortillas are delicious eaten hot with green salad but cold leftovers taste great in a sandwich with a dollop of mayonnaise or tomato ketchup. Always use boiled potatoes as the base of the dish but experiment with other ingredients such as spring onions, peas or chopped ham.

Serves 2

500g (1 lb) new potatoes, scrubbed
2 tablespoons olive oil
1 large red pepper, seeded and sliced
1 large onion, sliced
1 garlic clove, crushed
4 eggs, beaten
2 tablespoons milk
1 tablespoon chopped fresh parsley or 1 teaspoon dried seasoning

1 Cook the potatoes in boiling water for 10-15 minutes until just tender. Drain and slice.

2 Heat the oil in a small deep frying pan, preferably non-stick, and gently fry the pepper and onions together for about 8 minutes until very soft and lightly browned. Add the sliced potatoes and the garlic and cook for a further 5 minutes, stirring.

3 Beat together the eggs, milk, parsley and seasoning. Pour over the vegetables, turn down the heat to the lowest setting and cook gently for 5-8 minutes until the mixture is almost completely set.

4 Use a fish slice to carefully turn the tortilla over or if it's a little tricky, place a plate over the pan, invert the tortilla onto the plate and then slide it back into the pan. Cook for a further 2 or 3 minutes until the underside is golden brown. Cut into wedges and serve.

CHEESY POTATO PIE

REALLY EASY!

The credit for this recipe goes to a friend of mine who's still at college. She was adamant that I include this invention of hers as she eats it several times a week and it's still her favourite all-in-one meal.

Serves 2

500g (1 lb) potatoes, peeled and cubed
30g (1 oz) butter or margarine
2 tablespoons milk
1 tablespoon olive oil
1 onion, chopped
1 large leek, sliced
125g (4 oz) mushrooms, sliced
60g (2 oz) ham, cut into small squares
125g (4 oz) Cheddar cheese, grated
seasoning

1 Cook the potatoes in plenty of boiling salted water for 10-15 minutes until tender. Drain them well, return to the pan and mash together with the butter, milk and some seasoning.

2 Meanwhile, heat the oil in a large frying pan and cook the onion, leek and mushrooms together for 5 minutes. Add to the pan of mashed potatoes with the ham and half the cheese. Mix well and check the seasoning.

3 Transfer the mixture to a heatproof dish, sprinkle over the remaining cheese and place under a hot grill for 3-4 minutes until the cheese is bubbling and golden brown.

SPANISH TORTILLA • CHEESY POTATO PIE

CORNED BEEF HASH

R E A L L Y   E A S Y !

Corned beef hash is an amazing dish because it uses few ingredients and yet manages to taste great. Keep a can of corned beef in your cupboard for emergencies and you'll be able to knock up a filling supper in no time.

Serves 2

350g (12 oz) potatoes, unpeeled and cubed
200g (7 oz) can corned beef, roughly diced
2 tablespoons vegetable oil
few drops Tabasco or hot chilli sauce
seasoning

1 Cook the potatoes in boiling salted water for 10 or 15 minutes until tender. Drain well.

2 Heat the oil in a large frying pan and toss in the potatoes, corned beef, seasoning and Tabasco or hot chilli sauce. Mash together roughly with a fork and leave for 5 minutes so that the base develops a crust, Break up and turn the mixture with the fork and then leave again for a further 5 minutes so that it develops a new crust.

3 By now, the hash should be heated right through. Check the seasoning, adding a little more Tabasco or chilli sauce if liked and divide onto two warm plates. Serve with spaghetti hoops or baked beans for a complete meal.

TUNA FISH CAKES

R E A L L Y E A S Y !

Canned tuna works incredibly well in fish cakes. Make your own breadcrumbs by coarsely grating stale bread or if you have some handy, the ready-made, dried, golden breadcrumbs will work just as well. If the mixture feels a little too soft, allow it to cool completely before shaping.

Serves 2
350g (12 oz) potatoes, peeled and cubed
1 tablespoon mayonnaise
125g (4 oz) can of tuna in oil, drained
1 tablespoon chopped fresh parsley
1 small onion, finely chopped
1 egg, beaten
8 tablespoons breadcrumbs
2 tablespoons flour
vegetable oil for frying
seasoning

1 Cook the potatoes in plenty of boiling salted water for 10-15 minutes until tender. Drain them well, return to the pan and mash together with the mayonnaise.

2 Flake the the tuna fish and add to the mash with the parsley, chopped onion and season to taste. Mix well together.

3 With floured hands, shape the mixture into 4 large, flat, even-sized cakes. Dust lightly with flour, then dip into the beaten egg and then the breadcrumbs.

4 Heat a little oil in a frying pan and gently cook the fish cakes for about 5 minutes on each side until crisp and golden. Remove from the pan with a fish slice and drain on kitchen paper.

CORNED BEEF HASH • TUNA FISH CAKES

27

OCEAN PIE

EASY!

The fromage frais gives this dish a fresh, slightly sharper flavour than the usual fish pie. If you prefer, use the same quantity of milk instead.

Serves 2
*500g (1 lb) potatoes, peeled and cubed
knob of butter
2 tablespoons milk*

For The Filling
*Large fillet of smoked haddock or cod weighing about
250g (8 oz)
60g (2 oz) prawns
knob of butter
1 tablespoon flour
150 ml (¼ pint) milk
4 tablespoons natural fromage frais
30g (1 oz) frozen peas, thawed
1 tablespoon chopped fresh parsley
seasoning*

1 Preheat the oven to 200C, 400F, Gas 6. Cook the potatoes in boiling water for 10-15 minutes until tender. Drain well and mash with the butter, milk and a little seasoning.

2 Meanwhile, gently poach the fish fillet in boiling water for 5 minutes. Drain, carefully remove the skin and flake into bite-sized chunks. Arrange the fish, prawns and peas in the base of a deep heatproof dish.

3 To make the sauce, heat the butter in a small saucepan and when melted, add the flour. Stirring continuously, cook for 1 minute. Gradually add the milk, beating until it is all incorporated. Bring to the boil, toss in the parsley and season to taste.

4 Pour the sauce over the fish and then top with mashed potato. Bake for about 25 minutes until golden. Serve with broccoli or another green vegetable for a hearty supper.

OCEAN PIE

ROSTI WITH FRIED EGGS

REALLY EASY!

This is the best ever Sunday brunch. It takes minutes to make and is really filling, but it is fried in oil so don't eat it every day.

Serves 1
2 potatoes
2 eggs
seasoning
vegetable oil for frying

1 Peel the potatoes and grate coarsely into a bowl. Season with salt and pepper.

2 Heat a little oil in a frying pan, preferably non-stick. Tip the potatoes into the pan and flatten down with a fish slice. Cook over a fairly high heat until crisp and browned underneath. Turn over the rosti and cook for a further 3 minutes until browned on the second side.

3 Transfer to a warmed plate while you quickly fry the eggs in a little more oil. Top the rosti with the fried eggs and eat straightaway.

ROASTED SWEET POTATO & AUBERGINE SALAD

EASY!

Chunks of sweet potato, aubergine and peppers, roasted with garlic and oil and then tossed with cheese and wine vinegar just before serving.

Serves 2

1 large sweet potato, peeled and cut into chunks
1 large aubergine, cut into chunks
2 garlic cloves, halved
1 large red or orange pepper, cut into 2.5 cm (1 inch) squares
4 tablespoons olive oil
125g (4 oz) blue cheese eg Gorgonzola, Dolcellate, Stilton, diced
1 teaspoon wine vinegar or lemon juice
seasoning

1 Preheat the oven to 200C,400F,Gas 6. Place the sweet potato, aubergine, garlic cloves and pepper chunks in a roasting tin. Pour over the olive oil and sprinkle with salt. Roast in the oven, turning every quarter of an hour for 45 minutes until crisp and golden on the outside and cooked in the centre.

2 Turn the hot vegetables with any juices into a serving dish and allow to cool for about 5 minutes. Add the cheese dice and vinegar or lemon juice and toss well together. Check the seasoning and serve warm with garlic bread.

ROSTI & FRIED EGGS • ROASTED SWEET POTATO & AUBERGINE SALAD

LEEK AND POTATO SOUP

EASY!

 A thick, creamy soup of leek and potato with mint and crème fraîche.

Serves 2

30g (1 oz) butter
1 garlic clove, finely chopped
1 small dried red chilli, crushed
1 small onion, finely chopped
1 large leek, sliced
1 large potato diced
450 ml (¾ pint) vegetable stock
1 tablespoon chopped fresh mint or ½ teaspoon dried
3 tablespoons crème fraîche or single cream
seasoning

1 Melt the butter in a large saucepan and cook the garlic, chilli, onion, leek and potato for 5 minutes. Pour in the stock, bring to the boil and simmer covered for 30 minutes.

2 Add the mint, season and cook for a further 10 minutes. Sieve the soup through a metal strainer, working the cooked vegetables through the holes with a wooden spoon.

3 Return the soup to the pan, stir in the crème fraîche and gently heat through. Serve with warm crusty bread.

COTTAGE PIE

EASY!

Don't let the college refectory version put you off, as freshly made cottage pie tastes delicious.

Serves 2

500g (1 lb) potatoes, peeled and cubed
knob of butter
2 tablespoons milk
1 tablespoon vegetable oil
1 onion, finely chopped
250g (8 oz) lean minced beef
1 large carrot, diced
125g (4 oz) frozen peas, thawed
1 tablespoon tomato ketchup
1 teaspoon soy sauce
½ teaspoon dried mixed herbs
1 tablespoon chopped fresh parsley
seasoning

1 Preheat the oven to 200C,400F,Gas 6. Cook the potatoes in boiling water for 10-15 minutes until tender. Drain well and mash with the butter, milk and a little seasoning.

2 Heat the oil in a pan and fry the onion, mince, carrot and peas for 5 minutes. Add the ketchup, soy sauce, herbs and about 3 tablespoons of water. Cover and simmer gently for 20 minutes.

3 Check seasoning and transfer to a deep heatproof dish. Top with the mashed potato and bake for 25 minutes until golden.

BACON AND TOMATO LAYERED POTATO PIE

REALLY EASY!

A very tasty, inexpensive dish, that is great for cold winter evenings.

Serves 2

knob of butter or margarine
500g (1 lb) potatoes, very thinly sliced
1 small onion, thinly sliced
2 large tomatoes, thinly sliced
8 rashers, back bacon, chopped
150 ml (¼ pint) hot chicken stock
seasoning

1 Preheat the oven to 200C,400F,Gas 6. Generously butter a deep heat-proof casserole dish. Layer the potato, onion, tomato and bacon into the casserole dish, seasoning lightly between each layer, finishing with a layer of potato.

2 Carefully pour over the hot stock, dot with a little butter or margarine, and bake for 45 minutes until the top is lightly browned and the pie is cooked through.

SWEETCORN CHOWDER

REALLY EASY!

A chowder is traditionally a thick American soup. It often contains fish, but the name is usually given to any soup that is thickened with potato.

Serves 2

500g (1 lb) potatoes, peeled and diced
1 tablespoon vegetable oil
1 onion, chopped
4 rashers streaky bacon, chopped
1 small green chilli, finely chopped
1 red pepper, diced
600 ml (1 pint) milk
1 vegetable stock cube
125g (4 oz) natural fromage frais
400g (14 oz) can sweetcorn, drained
seasoning

1 Boil the potatoes in salted, boiling water for 10-15 minutes until tender.

2 Meanwhile, heat the oil in a large pan and fry the onion, bacon, chilli and pepper for 5 minutes until softened. Add the milk and the stock cube and simmer gently for 10 minutes.

3 Mash half the potato until smooth and stir into the soup with the rest of the diced potato and the sweetcorn. Simmer together for 10 minutes. Stir in the fromage frais, season to taste and serve with crusty bread.

BACON & TOMATO LAYERED POTATO PIE • SWEETCORN CHOWDER

POTATO FLAN WITH MUSHROOMS AND PEPPERS

E A S Y !

**This makes a delicious change to the usual
soggy-bottomed flans as it uses mashed potatoes
in place of the pastry.**

Serves 2

500g (1 lb) potatoes, peeled and cubed
knob of butter
2 tablespoons milk
2 tablespoons vegetable oil
1 red pepper, diced
1 small onion, chopped
125g (4 oz) mushrooms, thickly sliced
150 ml (¼ pint) milk
1 egg
60g (2 oz) Cheddar or other hard cheese, grated
seasoning

1 Cook the potatoes in boiling water for 10 - 15 minutes until tender. Drain well and mash with the butter, milk and a little seasoning.

2 Meanwhile, heat the oil in a large frying pan, add the pepper, onion and mushrooms and cook gently for about 8 minutes until softened and beginning to brown. Season well to taste.

3 Preheat the oven to 190C,375F,Gas 5. Brush a cake tin or small heatproof dish with oil. Using your fingers press the mashed potato mixture into the tin or dish until the base and sides are evenly covered.

4 Transfer the vegetables into the potato case. Beat together the milk, egg and a little seasoning. Pour over the vegetables and top with the grated cheese. Bake for 25-35 minutes until set.

MEDITERRANEAN CHICKEN AND POTATO STEW

REALLY EASY!

This is a cheery one-pot meal that will brighten up a chilly winter evening. Serve it with crusty bread to mop up all the juices.

Serves 2
1 tablespoon olive oil
2 chicken joints
2 garlic cloves, sliced
2 sprigs fresh thyme or ½ teaspoon dried
About 150 ml (¼ pint) water or stock
1 large potato, peeled and cubed
2 ripe tomatoes, chopped
seasoning

1 Heat the oil in a large saucepan, add the chicken, garlic and herbs and quickly fry for 5 minutes, until the chicken is lightly browned all over.

2 Add about 150 ml (¼ pint) of water or stock, cover and simmer gently for 15 minutes. Add the potatoes and tomatoes and cook for a further 15 minutes until the chicken is cooked through and the potatoes are tender. Season to taste and serve.

POTATO FLAN WITH MUSHROOMS & PEPPERS • CHICKEN & POTATO STEW

CLASSIC BAKED POTATO

REALLY EASY!

Baked potatoes make a great last-resort supper. A piping-hot stuffed potato is cheap, easy and nutritious, and the variety of fillings you can pile into a potato are endless. Choose an old main crop potato such as a King Edward rather than the new, thin skinned types. For a crunchy skin and floury, fluffy centre leave the potato in the oven for an extra 20 minutes, and for a softer skin, rub a little oil into the surface before cooking.

Serves 1
1 very large potato, weighing about 250g (8 oz)
small knob of butter
salt and freshly ground black pepper

1 Preheat the oven to 200C, 400F, Gas 6. Scrub the potato in clean, cold water and pat dry.

2 Pierce the potato a few times with a fork. Place directly onto the oven shelf and bake for an hour until soft. Cut open and serve with butter and a sprinkle of salt and pepper.

POTATO FILLINGS...

CHEESE AND HAM

**Use whatever cheese you have in the fridge
for this recipe.**

Serves 1

*1 hot baked potato
slice of boiled ham, chopped
60g (2 oz) cheese, grated
1 teaspoon English mustard
small knob of butter or margarine
seasoning*

1 Split the potato in half and scoop out the flesh to leave a hollow potato shell about 1 cm (½ inch) thick. Place the flesh in a bowl with the ham, cheese, mustard, butter and seasoning and mash well together.

2 Pile the filling back into the potato and return to the oven for 15 minutes until golden.

CLASSIC BAKED POTATO • POTATO FILLINGS... CHEESE & HAM

POTATO FILLINGS...

V SOFT CHEESE & WALNUTS

Soft cheese is readily available in supermarkets flavoured with garlic, herbs and pepper. With a little heat, it melts down to produce a delicious creamy sauce that works brilliantly as a pasta sauce or a topping for a hot potato.

Serves 1
1 hot baked potato
60g (2 oz) flavoured soft cheese, such as Boursin
1 tablespoon chopped walnuts

1 Cut a large cross into the potato and squeeze the potato to open it out. Pop in the soft cheese and sprinkle over the walnuts.

POTATO FILLINGS...

MOZZARELLA & PESTO SAUCE

**This recipe is based on the shop-bought,
commercial pesto, but if you are using your own,
home-made pesto (see recipe on page 53)
remember that it's not as strong, so you will need
more, but the taste will be well worth the effort.**

Serves 1
*1 hot baked potato
60g (2 oz) mozzarella cheese, grated
1 tablespoon pesto sauce
salt and freshly ground black pepper*

1 Cut a large cross into the potato and squeeze the potato to open it out. Mix together the mozzarella, pesto and a little seasoning. Spoon the mixture inside the potato and serve.

SOFT CHEESE & WALNUTS • MOZZARELLA & PESTO SAUCE

POTATO FILLINGS...

TUNA & GARLIC MAYONNAISE

**The wide variety of mayonnaise in the shops is
ever increasing. I think garlic mayonnaise goes
particularly well with tuna but you could choose
lemon, mustard or French.**

Serves 1
1 hot baked potato
125g (4 oz) can of tuna in oil, drained
2 tablespoons garlic mayonnaise
half a red onion or 3 spring onions, chopped
salt and freshly ground black pepper

1 Cut a large cross into the potato and squeeze the
potato to open it out. Mix together the tuna, mayonnaise, onions and season to taste. Spoon the mixture
inside the potato and sprinkle over a little black pepper.

SAUSAGE BOMBS

EASY!

This dish first appeared during war time when it was made with reconstituted dried potato, and known as 'pigs in blankets'!

Serves 2
500g (1 lb) potatoes, peeled and cubed
knob of butter
2 tablespoons milk
6 sausages
1 egg, beaten
125g (4 oz) fresh or dried golden breadcrumbs
seasoning
vegetable oil for frying

1 Cook the potatoes in boiling water for 10 - 15 minutes until tender. Drain well and mash with the butter, milk and a little seasoning.

2 Meanwhile fry the sausages for around 8 minutes, or until cooked through. Cover each sausage in a coat of mashed potato. Roll in egg and then in breadcrumbs.

3 Heat 5 cm (2 inches) of vegetable oil in a frying pan and cook the bombs, three at a time for 5 minutes or until crisp and golden. Drain on kitchen paper and serve with baked beans or spaghetti hoops.

TUNA & GARLIC MAYONNAISE • SAUSAGE BOMBS

43

PASTA

Pasta is simply hard flour blended into a firm dough with water and eggs. It is fairly easy to make fresh pasta yourself but it is time-consuming. When there are so many varieties of pasta you can buy cheaply and cook in a few minutes, opt for dried or ready-made fresh pasta.

INTRODUCTION

DRIED OR FRESH?

There are some people who claim that fresh pasta is by far superior to the dried. I don't agree. They are both equally good depending upon the sort of dish you want to create. Dried pasta is very cheap, can be stored easily for a long time and is firm with a good bite. If however, you fancy a filled pasta such as ravioli or tortellini, there are some very exciting fresh types around such as tomato ravioli filled with salmon and dill, that are well worth splashing out on for a special occasion. They usually cook in less than 5 minutes and just need tossing with a little warm cream for a super quick, but sophisticated supper.

COOKING

Pasta should be cooked in as a large a pan as possible so that it can move around freely and cook evenly. Bring a large pan of salted water to a rolling boil and add in the pasta, stir once and cook rapidly until tender with a firm bite. If you're cooking filled pasta shapes, the water should be simmered quite gently so that the parcels do not burst open.

SPAGHETTI ALLA CARBONNARA

REALLY EASY!

Vegetarians should use 180g (6 oz) sliced mushrooms in place of the chopped bacon for an equally tasty result.

Serves 2

250g (8 oz) spaghetti
1 tablespoon olive oil
1 small onion, chopped
1 garlic clove, finely chopped
4 slices of smoked streaky bacon, roughly chopped
2 eggs, beaten
150 ml (5 fl oz) carton single cream
2 tablespoons grated Parmesan cheese
salt and pepper

1 Cook the pasta in plenty of lightly salted boiling water for 10-12 minutes until tender. Meanwhile heat the oil in a small frying pan and cook the garlic, onion, and bacon for five minutes until golden. Beat together the eggs, cream, half of the Parmesan and a little seasoning.

2 Drain the pasta well and return to the pan. Quickly add the bacon mixture and the cream mixture and toss well together. Divide into two bowls, sprinkle over the remaining Parmesan and eat immediately.

PASTA WITH FRESH TOMATO AND MELTING MOZZARELLA

EASY!

This is a perfect summer time recipe which makes the most of the plump red tomatoes that are in abundance from about June.

Serves 2

4 large ripe tomatoes, halved
1 large onion, cut into 8 wedges
3 tablespoons olive oil
1 garlic clove, finely chopped
4 basil leaves, roughly chopped
125g (4 oz) mozzarella, cut into small dice
250g (8 oz) pasta
seasoning

1 Place the tomatoes skin side up with the onions on a baking sheet and drizzle over 2 tablespoons of the olive oil. Cook for about 8 minutes under a preheated grill, turning once, until golden brown and a little charred.

2 Heat the remaining oil in a small saucepan and fry the garlic for 2 minutes. Add the tomato mixture and the basil and season well to taste. Cover and simmer gently for 10 minutes or until pasta is ready.

3 Cook the pasta in plenty of boiling salted water until tender. Drain well and return to the pan. Toss in the sauce and mix well together. Sprinkle over the mozzarella and mix again, turn into bowls and serve immediately.

SPAGHETTI ALLA CARBONNARA • PASTA WITH FRESH TOMATO & MOZZARELLA

47

SPAGHETTI WITH ANCHOVIES, GARLIC AND CHILLI

REALLY EASY!

This is my all time favourite pasta dish. My mum always cooks it for me when I visit and I make it myself for friends at least once a week. For a more creamy consistency, after cooking the garlic, crush it with a heavy knife and whisk it back into the sauce.

Serves 2
250g (8 oz) spaghetti
4 tablespoons olive oil
4 garlic cloves, halved
1 red chilli, quartered
small can of anchovies in olive oil
freshly ground black pepper

1 Place a big pan of salted water on to boil. In a small saucepan heat the olive oil and gently cook the garlic and chilli pieces until golden and crisp. Be careful not to burn the garlic. Remove with a slotted spoon and set aside.

2 When the water is boiling, add in the pasta and cook until tender. Meanwhile add the can of anchovies, including the oil to the saucepan and cook for about 2 minutes. Now add 150 ml (¼ pint) of water and boil gently until the pasta is ready, whisking with a fork to break up the anchovies.

3 Drain the pasta well and return to the pan. Pour over the sauce and toss together. If it is too dry, add a little more olive oil or a couple of tablespoons of hot water. Divide between 2 bowls and sprinkle over plenty of black pepper. Sprinkle with the reserved garlic, and chilli if you wish.

PENNE WITH PEPPERS

REALLY EASY!

A very quick and filling dish of pasta with red peppers, garlic, basil and Parmesan.

Serves 2
2 large red peppers, cut into strips
2 garlic cloves, crushed
4 tablespoons olive oil
big handful fresh basil or parsley, roughly chopped
250g (8oz) penne (pasta quills)
2 tablespoons freshly grated Parmesan
salt and freshly ground black pepper

1 Heat the oil in a large frying pan and cook the peppers over a medium heat for at least 10 minutes until very soft. When you begin to cook them, they will steam as all the natural waters are released. The steaming subsides and the peppers turn a lovely caramel colour when they are ready.

2 Meanwhile, cook the pasta in plenty of boiling salted water until tender. Drain well and add to the frying pan. Toss in the herbs, Parmesan and plenty of seasoning. Mix well together, spoon into bowls and eat immediately.

SPAGHETTI BOLOGNESE

EASY!

Here is my version of this old favourite. You can use lamb or pork mince in place of beef, if you prefer.

Serves 2
1 tablespoon olive oil
1 onion, chopped
1 carrot, chopped
1 garlic clove, finely chopped
2 rashers streaky bacon, chopped
250g (8 oz) lean minced beef
400g (14 oz) can chopped tomatoes
1 teaspoon tomato purée
pinch of sugar
1 teaspoon dried mixed herbs
180g (6 oz) spaghetti
seasoning

1 Heat the oil in a saucepan and cook the onion, carrot, garlic and bacon for 5 minutes until softened. Add the mince and cook for a further 5 minutes until the meat has browned. Stir in the chopped tomatoes, purée, and herbs, cover and simmer for 20 minutes.

2 Meanwhile, cook the spaghetti in plenty of boiling, salted water until tender. Drain well and divide into 2 large bowls, making a well in the centre of each. Season the sauce with sugar, salt and pepper and spoon into the spaghetti nests. Serve immediately.

PASTA WITH CREAMY PRAWNS

REALLY EASY!

Spaghetti in a creamy, tomato sauce with prawns.

Serves 2

250g (8 oz) spaghetti or tagliatelle
150 ml (¼ pint) double cream
1 tablespoon tomato ketchup
1 teaspoon dried dill
1 garlic clove, finely chopped
125g (4 oz) large, cooked, peeled, prawns
seasoning

1 Cook the pasta in plenty of boiling salted water until tender.

2 Meanwhile, place the cream, tomato ketchup, dill, garlic and prawns together in a small saucepan. Heat gently and slowly bring to the boil. Remove from the heat and season to taste.

3 Drain the pasta well and return to the pan. Add the prawn sauce and toss with the pasta to coat. Turn into bowls and serve at once.

TAGLIATELLE WITH PESTO SAUCE

EASY!

If you're lucky enough to have a mini food processor, it will make short work of blending together the basil, pine nuts and garlic.

Serves 2
2 handfuls of fresh basil leaves
2 tablespoons pine nuts
2 garlic cloves
2 tablespoons olive oil
60g (2 oz) butter
60g (2 oz) freshly grated Parmesan
250g (8 oz) tagliatelle
seasoning

1 Place a big pan of salted water on to boil. Use a heavy knife to finely chop together the basil, pine nuts and garlic cloves until blended. Place the mixture in a small bowl and stir in the oil, butter and Parmesan.

2 When the water is boiling, toss in the pasta and cook until tender. Scoop out 2 tablespoons of hot water from the pasta pan and add to the pesto mixture. Drain the pasta and return to the pan.

3 Add the pesto and toss well together until thoroughly mixed. Season to taste and serve immediately with a little extra Parmesan scattered on top.

PASTA WITH CREAMY PRAWNS • TAGLIATELLE WITH PESTO SAUCE

CAULIFLOWER PASTA WITH CRISPY CRUMBS

E A S Y !

It is very important to use large pasta shapes in this recipe. The big tubes (rigatoni) are particularly good. A different, but very delicious way to eat cauliflower.

Serves 2

1 tablespoon olive oil
1 small onion, chopped
2 garlic cloves, finely chopped
200g (7 oz) can chopped tomatoes
1 tablespoon chopped fresh parsley or 1 teaspoon dried
1 small cauliflower, cut into florets
180g (6 oz) large pasta tubes, shells or bows

For The Topping

1 tablespoon olive oil
4 tablespoons fresh white breadcrumbs
seasoning

1 Place a big pan of salted water on to boil. Heat the oil in a small pan and fry the onion and garlic together for 5 minutes until softened. Add the tomatoes and parsley and season to taste. Cover and simmer very gently until the pasta is ready.

2 Toss the cauliflower and pasta into the pan of boiling water and cook together for around 12 minutes until the pasta is tender and the cauliflower is soft.

3 Meanwhile heat the remaining oil in a frying pan, add the breadcrumbs and stir-fry for 5 minutes or so, until crisp and golden brown.

4 Drain the pasta and cauliflower well and return to the pan. Stir in the tomato sauce and mix thoroughly together. The cauliflower will break up and blend with the tomato sauce. Divide into serving bowls and sprinkle over the crispy crumbs. Serve straightaway.

TAGLIATELLE WITH MEATBALLS

EASY!

Tiny meat balls in a tomato sauce served on pasta nests.

Serves 2
250g (8 oz) minced beef
60g (2 oz) fresh white breadcrumbs
1 tablespoon freshly grated Parmesan
1 egg, beaten
1 tablespoon chopped fresh parsley
1 tablespoon olive oil
1 small onion, chopped
1 garlic clove, chopped
400g (14 oz) can chopped tomatoes
1 tablespoon chopped fresh basil or 1 teaspoon dried
250g (8 oz) tagliatelle

1 Place the minced beef, breadcrumbs, Parmesan, egg, parsley and a little seasoning in a bowl and mix together. Shape into about 12 small balls.

2 Heat the olive oil in a large saucepan and cook the onion, garlic and meatballs for 5 minutes until the meatballs are browned all over. Add the tomatoes and basil and season to taste. Simmer, covered for about 20 minutes.

3 Meanwhile, cook the tagliatelle in plenty of boiling, salted water until tender. Drain well and divide into 2 large bowls, making a well in the centre of each. Spoon the meatballs and tomato sauce into the pasta nests and serve sprinkled with a little extra Parmesan.

PASTA SPIRALS WITH BUTTERY COURGETTES

REALLY EASY!

Pasta spirals tossed with tender courgette sticks and served with Parmesan.

Serves 2

2 small courgettes
30g (1 oz) butter
1 tablespoon olive oil
2 garlic cloves, finely chopped
½ teaspoon dried rosemary
250g (8 oz) pasta spirals
seasoning
1 tablespoon freshly grated Parmesan

1 Place a big pan of salted water on to boil. Slice each courgette lengthwise into four strips. Place the strips on top of each other and slice lengthwise into thin sticks. Cut them widthways to make small sticks.

2 Heat the butter and oil together and cook the garlic, courgettes and rosemary over a fairly high heat for about 7 - 8 minutes until the courgettes are golden brown. Season to taste.

3 Meanwhile cook the pasta in plenty of boiling salted water until tender. Drain well and return to the pan. Add the courgette mixture and toss together. Divide into serving dishes and sprinkle over the Parmesan.

PASTA AND AUBERGINE LAYER

E A S Y !

This recipe not only tastes delicious but also looks quite impressive. It's a perfect supper dish if you're entertaining, and if you feel like splashing out, use a handful of fresh basil leaves in place of the dried.

Serves 2
250g (8 oz) pasta shapes
1 large aubergine
1 tablespoon olive oil
400g (14 oz) can of chopped tomatoes
1 teaspoon dried basil
125g (4 oz) mozzarella cheese, grated
1 tablespoon grated Parmesan cheese
salt and pepper

1 Preheat the oven to 200C,400F,Gas 6. Cook the pasta in plenty of lightly salted boiling water for about 12 minutes or until just tender.

2 Meanwhile, slice the aubergine into thick rounds, brush with the olive oil and sprinkle lightly with a little salt. Place under a preheated grill for 6-8 minutes until golden brown on both sides and soft in the centre.

3 Drain the pasta well and return to the pan. Add the can of tomatoes and basil, mix to combine and season to taste.

4 Spoon one third of the pasta mixture into the base of a heat proof dish. Arrange half of the aubergine slices on top of the pasta and sprinkle over half of the mozzarella. Repeat to make a second layer, finishing with the final third of pasta.

5 Sprinkle over the Parmesan, and bake for 15-20

minutes until the pasta has a golden brown crust and is piping hot. If the top browns too quickly, cover with a lid or foil.

PASTA WITH TUNA AND MUSHROOMS

REALLY EASY!

Serves 2
250g (8 oz) pasta shapes
1 onion, chopped
1 garlic clove, sliced
1 tablespoon olive oil
198g (7oz) can tuna in oil, drained
180g (6 oz) button mushrooms, sliced
2 tablespoons chopped fresh parsley
salt and freshly ground black pepper

1 Cook the pasta in plenty of boiling salted water until tender. Meanwhile fry the onion and garlic in the oil for 5 minutes until softened.

2 Add the tuna and mushrooms and 150ml (¼ pint) of water and cook gently for 10 minutes or until the pasta is cooked. Stir in parsley and season to taste.

3 Drain the pasta and return to the pan. Tip in sauce and toss well together. Divide into bowls and serve with a good sprinkling of black pepper on each.

MINESTRONE SOUP

REALLY EASY!

Don't feel tied to this recipe. Chop and change the vegetables to suit your storecupboard. The word 'minestrone', simply means big soup, but it almost always has pasta in it. Use pastina, tiny pasta shapes specially made for soups, or break strands of spaghetti into very short lengths.

Serves 2-3
1 tablespoon olive oil
4 rashers of streaky bacon, chopped
1 small onion, chopped
1 garlic clove, chopped
1 carrot, diced
1 courgette, diced
1 small potato, diced
1 celery stick, diced
2 tomatoes, diced
900 ml (1½ pints) vegetable stock
60g (2 oz) pastina
1 tablespoon chopped fresh parsley
1 tablespoon freshly grated Parmesan
seasoning

1 Heat the olive oil in a large saucepan. Fry together the bacon, onion, garlic, carrot, courgette, potato and celery for 5 minutes. Add the tomatoes and stock, cover and simmer for 1 hour.

2 Stir in the pastina and parsley and cook for 10 minutes until pastina is tender. Check seasoning, ladle into bowls, sprinkle with Parmesan and serve.

CRAIG'S MACARONI CHEESE

EASY!

Macaroni cheese is a student classic as it's so filling and simple to make. When I first met eternal student Craig, he cooked me this every single time I went round for supper. Fortunately, I've taught him a thing or two since!

Serves 2
250g (8 oz) macaroni
30g (1 oz) butter or margarine
1 small onion, chopped
1 garlic clove, crushed
30g (1 oz) flour
300ml (½ pint) milk
180g (6 oz) mature Cheddar, grated
1 tablespoon wholegrain mustard
seasoning

1 Cook the pasta in plenty of boiling salted water until tender. Meanwhile, heat the butter in a saucepan and gently cook the onion and garlic for 5 minutes until softened.

2 Stir the flour into the pan and blend into the butter and onions with a wooden spoon. Gradually beat in the milk to make a smooth sauce. If it does become lumpy, whisk it vigorously.

3 Bring gently to the boil and add 125g (4 oz) of the cheese, and the mustard. Heat gently for a couple of minutes, until the cheese melts and season to taste.

4 Drain the pasta and return to the pan. Pour in the sauce and mix well, then transfer to a heat proof dish, scatter over the remaining cheese and pop under a preheated grill for 5 minutes until golden and bubbling.

(35)

CHICKEN AND SWEETCORN NOODLE SOUP

REALLY EASY!

Chinese-style egg soups such as this one are really easy to make at home. If you like, try chopping up some crab sticks and adding them at step 2 in place of the chicken.

Serves 2

1 tablespoon vegetable oil
1 chicken breast, skinned and cut into small pieces
1 garlic clove, sliced
125g (4 oz) sweetcorn kernels
1 tablespoon cornflour
600 ml (1 pint) chicken or vegetable stock
60g (2 oz) vermicelli pasta
1 egg
1 tablespoon fresh lemon juice
seasoning

1 Heat the oil in a large pan and gently cook the garlic and chicken for 5 minutes until the chicken is white.

2 Blend the cornflour with a little of the stock and add to the pan with the remaining stock, the sweetcorn, and vermicelli. Bring to the boil, stirring continuously and simmer for 5 minutes.

3 Beat together the the egg and lemon juice and slowly trickle into the pan, stirring with a chopstick or fork to make egg strands. Season to taste and serve immediately.

CRAIG'S MACARONI CHEESE • CHICKEN & SWEETCORN NOODLE SOUP

PASTA WITH WALNUTS AND CORIANDER

REALLY EASY!

This creamy dish is amazingly quick and easy to prepare. Add a bit of variety to the dish by experimenting with different nuts such as hazelnuts, almonds or even peanuts.

Serves 2
250g (8 oz) pasta
1 tablespoon olive oil
125g (4 oz) cream cheese
60g (2 oz) Gruyère or Cheddar cheese
60g (2 oz) chopped walnuts
2 tablespoons chopped fresh coriander
salt and freshly ground black pepper

1 Cook the pasta in plenty of lightly salted boiling water for about 12 minutes, or until tender.

2 Meanwhile, beat together the olive oil, cream cheese, Gruyère, walnuts, coriander and plenty of seasoning.

3 Drain the pasta, toss in the cheese mixture and mix well together for 1 or 2 minutes until the cheese melts and coats the pasta. Divide into 2 bowls and serve with a sprinkling of black pepper and coriander.

PASTA SHELLS WITH BROCCOLI AND LEMON

REALLY EASY!

This is a very quick dish, make it even quicker and use frozen broccoli florets in place of fresh, if you wish. Pre-packed broccoli in supermarkets can often be quite expensive, so if you are near any market stalls, always check out the price - you'll find it is often cheaper and you can buy the exact amount you want.

Serves 2
180g (6 oz) pasta shells
250g (8 oz) broccoli florets
knob of butter or margarine
1 tablespoon flour
200 ml (7 fl oz) vegetable stock
grated rind and juice of half a lemon
seasoning

1 Cook the pasta in plenty of lightly salted boiling water for 7 minutes. Add the broccoli to the pan and cook together for a further 5 minutes until both pasta and broccoli are tender.

2 Meanwhile, heat the butter in a small pan, add the flour and beat together with a wooden spoon until smooth. Gradually stir in the stock, bring to to the boil and season to taste. Add the lemon juice and rind and simmer gently for 1 minute.

3 Drain the pasta. Pour over the sauce, toss well together and serve.

PASTA WITH WALNUTS & CORIANDER • PASTA SHELLS WITH BROCCOLI & LEMON

FARFALLE FLORENTINA

EASY!

If you ever see Florentine or Florentina on a menu, it means the dish originates from Florence in Italy - although there's no guarantee that it's true, you can be sure that the dish will contain spinach and usually cheese.

Serves 2
2 tablespoons olive oil
1 small onion, finely chopped
2 garlic cloves, finely chopped
1 small hot chilli, chopped (optional)
400g (14 oz) can of chopped tomatoes
1 teaspoon honey or sugar
1 tablespoon chopped fresh parsley, or 1 teaspoon dried
250g (8 oz) farfalle (pasta bows)
250g (8 oz) spinach, thawed if frozen
125g (4 oz) mozzarella cheese, sliced
1 tablespoon freshly grated Parmesan
seasoning

1 Place a large saucepan of salted water on to boil. Heat 1 tablespoon of oil in a small saucepan and gently fry the onion, garlic and chilli, if using, for 5 minutes until softened. Stir in the tomatoes, honey and parsley, season to taste, cover and simmer for 10 minutes or until the pasta is ready.

2 Cook the pasta bows for 10-12 minutes until tender. Meanwhile, if using fresh spinach, cook it in a little boiling water for 5 minutes , until wilted. Drain the spinach well and stir into the tomato sauce – if using frozen spinach, you won't need to cook it, just stir it directly into the sauce.

3 Drain the pasta and return to the pan, pour over the sauce and toss well together. Turn into a heatproof dish and sprinkle over the mozzarella, Parmesan and remaining tablespoon of olive oil. Place under a preheated grill for 5 minutes until the cheese is bubbling and golden.

TAGLIATELLE WITH MUSHROOM SAUCE

REALLY EASY!

This is really a cheats' dish but if you're pushed for time, you can turn out a hearty meal with very little effort.

Serves 2
1 tablespoon olive oil
1 small onion, finely chopped
1 garlic clove, finely chopped
2 rashers of streaky bacon, chopped
125g (4 oz) mushrooms, sliced
150 ml (¼ pint) can of condensed cream of mushroom soup
1 tablespoon chopped fresh parsley
250g (8 oz) tagliatelle
1 tablespoon freshly grated Parmesan, to serve (optional)
seasoning

1 Place a large saucepan of salted water on to boil. Heat the oil in a small saucepan and gently fry the onion, garlic and bacon for 5 minutes, until softened.

2 Add the mushrooms and cook for a further 2 minutes. Stir in the soup, season to taste and simmer for 10 minutes, or until the pasta is ready.

3 Cook the pasta for 10 - 12 minutes until tender. Drain well and divide into two bowls. Stir the parsley into the sauce and pour over the pasta. Serve immediately with a good sprinkling of black pepper and freshly grated Parmesan.

RICE & GRAINS

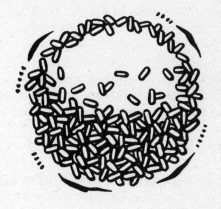

Cheap, nutritious and very easy to cook, rice is
the staple diet in many countries. It thrives on
waterlogged, marshy soil where other cereals,
such as wheat will not grow.

INTRODUCTION

Although there are literally hundreds of different rices, there are only two basic grains, long and round. Round rice is stirred during cooking to release the starch and produce a creamy, slightly sticky rice which is perfect for things like milk puddings, risottos or sushi. Long grain rices stay separate and should be washed well before cooking and not stirred whilst being cooked.

COOKING RICE

There are two very good methods of boiling long grain rice. I normally go for the straightforward Open Pan method but the Absorption technique is just as successful.

Open Pan Method

Bring a large pan of salted boiling water to the boil. Tip in the rice, stir once and simmer fairly rapidly, uncovered, until the rice is tender. Drain in a sieve and turn out onto a large plate for 2 minutes to allow the grains to dry and separate.

Absorption Method

After weighing the rice tip it into a measuring jug or a mug and take note of the volume before transferring to a saucepan. Now measure twice that volume in cold water and add to the pan with a teaspoon of salt. Bring to the boil, lower the heat to a slow simmer, cover tightly and cook for 15-20 minutes for long grain rice, 10 minutes for basmati and 35-45 minutes for brown.

RICE TYPES

Risotto Rice

Risotto rice is a plump, longish, round grain that absorbs lots of liquid and cooks easily without becoming mushy. If stirred frequently during cooking, it gives a very creamy texture. The best risotto rice is Arborio. It is a bit expensive, and in my experience all the risotto rices are good.

Long grain white rice

This is a polished rice that, like most other white rices including risotto and basmati, has had its husk and bran removed. It can be boiled using either of the two methods above or used for biryani or other oven baked savoury rices where separate grains are preferred.

Basmati rice

This is a very delicate, long, slim, fragrant grain that is used extensively in Indian cookery. It is relatively expensive and can be replaced by the usual long grain rice if preferred. It should be washed very well several times and soaked in warm water for 20 minutes before cooking. After soaking it must be handled carefully as the grains are fragile and can easily break. Cook by either of the methods described for just 10 minutes or use for aromatic pilau or spiced rice dishes.

Brown rice

Brown rice is a long grain rice which has only had the very tough husk removed, and the bran left intact. It has a nutty flavour and quite chewy texture, but because of the tough layer, takes about 35-45 minutes to cook and absorbs a lot more water than white. It is however, not only one of the most flavoursome rices but also the most nutritious.

There are lots of other grains and cereals that are used for cooking world wide. Experiment with different grains, both whole and milled; see vegetable couscous (page 82) and Cornbread Chilli Pie (page 86) for more ideas.

KEDGEREE

REALLY EASY!

Kedgeree is traditionally served for breakfast, and is guaranteed to get you back on your feet after a night out on the tiles. If you can't face it first thing in the morning, it makes a great supper dish.

Serves 2

250g (8 oz) long grain rice
2 smoked, peppered mackerel fillets, flaked
30g (1 oz) butter or margarine
2 hard boiled eggs, shelled and roughly chopped
1 tablespoon roughly chopped parsley
4 tablespoons single cream (optional)
seasoning

1 Rinse the rice well with cold water. Place in a large saucepan and pour in enough cold water to rise about an inch higher than the rice. Stir once only, bring to the boil and simmer for about 15-20 minutes, until the rice is cooked. Drain well in a sieve and set aside for a few minutes for the grains to separate

2 Melt the butter in a large frying pan. Add rice, flaked fish, eggs, parsley, cream if using, and season to taste.

To hard boil an egg – Plunge the egg into a pan of boiling water. Boil steadily over a medium heat for 12 minutes. Run under cold water until egg is completely cold to prevent the yolk turning grey.

MUSHROOM RISOTTO

REALLY EASY!

V A good risotto should be creamy with soft but not mushy grains. It might take a couple of attempts to get right, but once you have it perfected, there is no end to the variations you can develop yourself. Try using canned or sun dried tomatoes, different herbs or green vegetables. If you feel like treating yourself, substitute a glass of wine (white or red) for some of the stock.

Serves 2
1 tablespoon olive oil
1 small onion, finely chopped
1 garlic clove, crushed
250g (8 oz) risotto rice
250g (8 oz) flat mushrooms, sliced
900 ml (1½ pints) vegetable stock
30g (1 oz) butter
2 tablespoons freshly grated Parmesan
2 tablespoons chopped, fresh parsley
seasoning

1 Heat the oil in a large pan and gently fry the onion and garlic for 5 minutes until softened. Stir in the rice and mushrooms and cook together for 1 minute.

2 Gradually add the stock a little at a time, waiting for the liquid to be absorbed before adding any more, until all the liquid is absorbed and the rice is cooked. Keep the rice over a fairly high heat, stir it frequently and it should take 20 minutes. If it takes longer than this, the rice will become too soft, so don't be afraid to raise the heat.

3 When the rice is cooked, stir in the butter, Parmesan and parsley. Season to taste and serve immediately.

PAELLA

EASY!

Creamy rice with chicken and seafood, this dish, made in larger quantities, is great for a party.

Serves 2
1 tablespoon vegetable oil
1 small onion, chopped
1 garlic clove, chopped
2 chicken drumsticks
600 ml (1 pint) vegetable or chicken stock
180g (6 oz) short grain or risotto rice
2 tomatoes, roughly chopped
250g (8 oz) fresh seafood eg prawns, cod, mussels, squid,
all cut into bite-sized pieces or 125g (4 oz) ready-
prepared seafood cocktail
60g (2 oz) frozen peas
1 tablespoon chopped fresh parsley
seasoning

1 Heat the oil in a large pan and fry the onion, garlic and chicken for about 5 minutes. Add the stock, cover and simmer for 15 minutes.

2 Add the rice and tomatoes and cook, covered for 20 minutes, stirring regularly. If using raw fish add to the pan after 10 minutes cooking time, if using seafood cocktail add after 15 minutes.

3 When the rice and chicken are cooked, stir in the peas and parsley and cook for a further 2 minutes. Season to taste and serve.

MUSHROOM RISOTTO • PAELLA

BROCCOLI AND ALMOND PILAF

REALLY EASY!

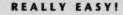 A brown rice pilaf with a hint of curry, containing broccoli, onion, mushrooms and topped with toasted flaked almonds.

Serves 2
1 tablespoon olive oil
1 small onion, chopped
250g (8 oz) easy-cook brown rice
1 teaspoon curry paste
450ml (¾ pint) vegetable stock
250g (8 oz) broccoli, broken into florets
250g (8 oz) button mushrooms, halved
30g (1 oz) toasted flaked almonds
seasoning

1 Heat the oil in a large frying pan. Stir-fry the onion, mushrooms and curry paste for 5 minutes. Add the rice and stir for a further minute.

2 Pour in the stock and bring to the boil. Stir once, then cover and simmer for 30 minutes. Add the broccoli and mushrooms, cover and simmer for a further 10 minutes. Season to taste and serve sprinkled with flaked almonds.

LEMON CHICKEN RICE

REALLY EASY!

Very easy dish of chicken pieces cooked on a bed of lemon flavoured rice.

Serves 2
250g (8 oz) long grain rice
juice and grated rind of a lemon
1 tablespoon chopped fresh parsley
1 garlic clove, finely chopped
2 chicken pieces, skinned
small knob of butter
600ml (1 pint) chicken stock
seasoning

1 Preheat the oven to 180C, 350F, Gas 4. Place the rice, lemon rind, parsley, garlic and a little seasoning in a large bowl and mix well together. Tip into a large roasting tin.

2 Spread the butter over the chicken pieces, sprinkle lightly with salt and pepper and press firmly into the bed of rice.

3 Mix together the lemon juice and stock and pour over the rice and chicken. Cover with foil and bake for 1 hour, until the chicken is cooked through and the rice is tender.

BROCCOLI & ALMOND PILAF • LEMON CHICKEN RICE

77

LAMB BIRYANI

EASY!

Biryani is traditionally a lamb dish but it needn't be – try a vegetable or chicken version of your own.

Serves 2-3
1 tablespoon vegetable oil
1 onion, chopped
1 garlic clove, finely chopped
500g (1 lb) lean lamb, cubed
2 tablespoons mild curry paste
150 ml (¼ pint) natural yogurt
1 teaspoon ground turmeric
180g (6 oz) long grain rice
seasoning

1 Heat the oil in a saucepan and fry the onion, garlic and lamb for 5 minutes until lightly browned. Stir in the curry paste and yogurt, season to taste, cover with a lid and simmer gently for 30 minutes.

2 Meanwhile, boil 600ml (1 pint) of water in a large saucepan. Wash the rice well and add to the pan with the turmeric and a teaspoon of salt. Cook without stirring for 15 - 20 minutes until the rice is just tender.

3 Preheat the oven to 180C,350F,Gas 4. Generously butter a casserole dish and spoon in half the rice. Arrange the lamb curry on top and finish with a layer of the remaining rice. Cover with foil and bake for 30 minutes.

CHINESE EGG-FRIED RICE

EASY!

The secret of egg-fried rice is to cook the egg separately. If you add raw egg to the hot rice whilst in the pan, it will simply absorb the egg and become sticky.

Serves 2
180g (6 oz) long grain rice
2 tablespoons vegetable oil
2 eggs, beaten
1 chicken breast, shredded
1 cm (½ inch) piece fresh ginger, grated
1 carrot, cut into matchsticks
bunch of spring onions, thickly sliced on the diagonal
125g (4 oz) can sliced water chestnuts
60g (2 oz) prawns
1 tablespoon soy sauce

1 Wash the rice well and cook in boiling water for 15-20 minutes until tender. Drain well.

2 Heat a little of the oil in a wok or large frying pan. Tip in the beaten eggs and using a chop stick, stir until set. Remove from the wok and set aside.

3 Heat the remaining vegetable oil in the wok and quickly stir-fry the chicken, ginger, and carrot sticks for 5 minutes over a high heat until the chicken is cooked through.

4 Stir in the spring onions, water chestnuts, cooked rice and egg, mixing well together. Season with soy sauce, continue stir-frying until heated right through and serve.

BAKED TOMATO RICE CAKE

EASY

V Give a new lease of life to left over risotto by turning it into a baked rice cake. Use any type of risotto, such as the mushroom risotto on page 74 or like the one below, tomato. Cut the cake into wedges and serve with salad.

Serves 2

1 tablespoon olive oil
1 small onion, finely chopped
1 garlic clove, crushed
250g (8 oz) risotto rice
8 sun dried tomatoes in oil, finely shredded
400g (14 oz) can of chopped tomatoes
900 ml (1½ pints) vegetable stock
30g (1 oz) butter
2 tablespoons freshly grated Parmesan
2 tablespoons chopped, fresh parsley
2 eggs
150 ml (¼ pint) milk
125g (4 oz) mozzarella cheese, cubed
seasoning

1 Heat the oil in a large pan and gently fry the onion and garlic for 5 minutes until softened. Stir in the rice and sun dried tomatoes and cook together for 1 minute.

2 Tip in the can of tomatoes and stir until the juices are absorbed by the rice. Gradually add the stock a little at a time, waiting for the liquid to be absorbed before adding any more, until the rice is cooked. Keep the rice over a fairly high heat, stir it frequently and it should take 20 minutes.

3 When the rice is cooked, stir in the butter, Parmesan and parsley and season to taste. Leave the risotto to cool for 5 minutes.

4 Preheat the oven to 180C,350F,Gas 4. Turn the mixture into a deep cake tin. Beat together the eggs and milk, season lightly and pour over the mixture. Sprinkle on the mozzarella and use a chopstick or a fork to loosely blend the mixture together. Bake for 25 minutes until set.

BAKED TOMATO RICE CAKE

VEGETABLE COUSCOUS

EASY!

 Couscous is a typical Middle Eastern ingredient. Although often used in the same way as other grains, it is actually derived from the root of the cassava plant, and is related to semolina.

Serves 2

180g (6 oz) couscous
2 tablespoons vegetable oil
1 onion, roughly chopped
1 garlic clove, finely chopped
1 small aubergine, cubed
1 carrot, sliced
½ teaspoon ground cumin
2 tomatoes, chopped
1 tablespoon tomato purée
300 ml (½ pint) vegetable stock
200g (7 oz) can chickpeas, drained
1 tablespoon chopped fresh coriander
60g (2 oz) peanuts
seasoning

1 Put the couscous in a bowl and cover with boiling water for 10 minutes until it has swollen.

2 Meanwhile, heat the oil in a saucepan and cook the onion, garlic, aubergine, carrots and cumin for 5 minutes. Stir in the tomatoes, purée, vegetable stock and chickpeas and bring to the boil.

3 Line a metal sieve with a new paper kitchen cloth or a very clean tea towel and place over the pan. Tip in the couscous. Cover the pan with foil, to enclose the steam and simmer very gently for 25 minutes until the vegetables are tender.

4 Fluff up the couscous with a fork and divide onto

plates. Stir the chopped coriander and peanuts into the vegetables and season to taste. Spoon onto the bed of couscous and serve.

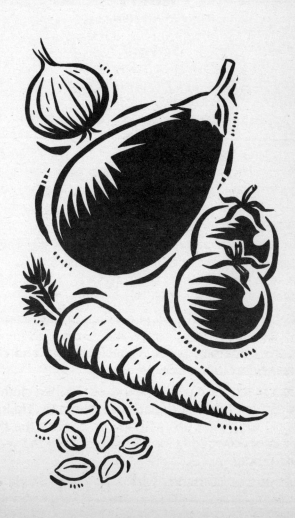

RASTAFARIAN RICE AND PEAS

REALLY EASY!

Rice and Peas is a traditional Rastafarian dish, though to really eat rasta, to be 'irie' (at one with nature), you should shun any additives, or processed foods, which means no canned beans and no salt!

Serves 2
250g (8 oz) brown rice
150 ml (¼ pint) coconut milk
½ teaspoon dried thyme
400g (14 oz) can black-eye beans, drained
seasoning

1 Wash the rice well and place in a large saucepan with the coconut milk, thyme and 300 ml (½ pint) water. Bring to the boil, cover and simmer gently for 15 minutes.

2 Add the beans, season to taste and cook together for a further 10 minutes until the rice is tender.

35

TABBOULEH

REALLY EASY!

V

This classic Lebanese salad is based on bulgar wheat, also labelled as cracked wheat. When you buy it in the shops, it has already been cooked and then dried so it just needs rehydrating with a little boiling water. Keep it cool and dry in your cupboard and it will last for months.The addition of Greek feta cheese makes tabbouleh taste even better. Eat with warm pitta bread or use it to stuff hollowed-out beef tomatoes.

Serves 2
125g (4 oz) bulgar wheat
2 tomatoes, chopped
4 spring onions, sliced
125g (4 oz) feta cheese, crumbled or diced
2-3 tablespoons finely chopped parsley
juice of a lemon
3 tablespoons olive oil
seasoning

1 Put the bulgar wheat in a large bowl and fill with boiling water. Set aside for 20 minutes until the grains have swollen and absorbed most of the water. Drain very well and return to the bowl.

2 Stir in the tomatoes, onions, feta, parsley, lemon juice and olive oil. Mix well together, season to taste and serve.

RASTAFARIAN RICE & PEAS • TABBOULEH

CORNBREAD CHILLI PIE

EASY!

 Cornmeal is the basis of many dishes, from the Northern Italian speciality 'polenta' to this favourite of southern USA.

Serves 2
1 tablespoon sunflower or vegetable oil
1 onion, chopped
2 garlic cloves, finely chopped
2 hot chillies, finely chopped
1 green pepper, diced
400g (14 oz) can red kidney beans, drained
400g (14 oz) can chopped tomatoes
few drops of Tabasco or other hot chilli sauce
seasoning

For The Cornbread
125g (4 oz) fine cornmeal
1 tablespoon plain flour
½ teaspoon salt
2 teaspoons baking powder
1 egg, beaten
6 tablespoons milk
1 tablespoon sunflower or vegetable oil

1 Preheat the oven to 220C,425F,Gas 7. Heat the oil and fry the onion, garlic, chillies and pepper for 5 minutes until softened. Add the kidney beans, tomatoes, Tabasco and season to taste.Bring to the boil and simmer for 10 minutes.

2 Place the cornmeal, flour, salt and baking powder in a bowl and make a well in the centre. Add the egg, milk and vegetable oil and mix well together with a wooden spoon.

3 Transfer the chilli mixture to a deep baking dish and

spoon on top the cornbread mixture. Smooth the top with the back of a spoon and bake for 25 minutes until firm.

NASI GORENG

EASY!

Nasi Goreng is Indonesian in origin. Serve it with prawn crackers.

Serves 2
180g (6 oz) long grain rice
2 tablespoons vegetable oil
6 spring onions, sliced
1 garlic clove, finely chopped
250g (8oz) lean beef or pork, cut into thin strips
1 teaspoon chilli powder
2 tablespoons soy sauce
small knob of butter or 1 tablespoon vegetable oil
2 eggs, beaten
seasoning

1 Wash the rice well and cook in boiling water for 15 - 20 minutes until tender. Drain well.

2 Meanwhile, heat the oil in large frying pan and cook the onion, garlic and meat for 8 minutes until the vegetables have softened and the meat is cooked through. Stir in the cooked rice, chilli powder and soy sauce. Stir fry for 5 minutes until piping hot and turn into serving bowls.

3 Melt the butter in the same frying pan and pour in the beaten egg. Cook for a minute or two on each side and turn out onto a chopping board. Roll up the omelette and cut into slices. Arrange the slices on top of the rice and serve.

APPLEY RICE SALAD

REALLY EASY!

A fresh tasting rice salad with apples, cheese, onion and red peppers.

Serves 2
180g (6 oz) long grain rice
2 green apples
juice and grated rind of a lime
1 red onion, finely chopped
125g (4 oz) cheese, eg Cheddar, Edam, diced
1 red pepper, diced
2 tablespoons olive oil
1 tablespoon chopped fresh coriander or parsley
seasoning

1 Wash the rice well and cook in boiling water for 15-20 minutes until tender. Drain well and set aside to go cold.

2 Meanwhile, dice and core the apples and toss in the lime juice. Place in a large bowl with the red onion, cheese, red pepper, olive oil, rice, herbs and seasoning. Toss well together and serve.

NASI GORENG • APPLEY RICE SALAD

JAMBALAYA

REALLY EASY!

Jambalaya has no rules. Try adding different vegetables, pieces of cooked chicken or bacon for an equally tasty result.

Serves 2

1 tablespoon vegetable oil
1 garlic clove
1 onion, chopped
1 small hot chilli, chopped
1 red pepper, diced
2 Pepperami salami sausages, cut into 1cm (½ inch) thick slices
150g (5 oz) long grain white rice
2 large tomatoes, diced
300 ml (½ pint) vegetable or chicken stock
2 tablespoons chopped fresh parsley
seasoning

1 Heat the oil in a large pan and gently cook the garlic, onion, chilli and pepper for 5 minutes, until softened.

2 Add the salami, rice, tomatoes and stock, bring to the boil, cover and simmer for 15 - 20 minutes until the rice is tender and the liquid has been absorbed.

3 Stir in the parsley and season to taste. Serve immediately.

CAJUN GUMBO

EASY!

Like Jambalaya, there is no one way to make a gumbo; as long as it's fairly fiery and contains prawns and okra (also known as ladies fingers), it qualifies.

Serves 2

1 tablespoon vegetable oil
2 rashers streaky bacon
1 chicken breast, cut into small pieces
1 small onion, sliced
250g (8 oz) fresh okra, sliced in half lengthways
400g (14 oz) can chopped tomatoes
150ml (¼ pint) chicken stock
125g (4 oz) long grain white rice
125g (4 oz) prawns
1-2 tablespoons chopped, fresh coriander
few drops of Tabasco or other hot chilli sauce
seasoning

1 Heat the oil in a large saucepan and gently fry together the bacon, chicken and onion for 5 minutes. Add the okra and stir fry for a further 3 minutes.

2 Add the can of tomatoes and the stock and bring to the boil. Season to taste and simmer, covered for 15 minutes until the okra is tender and the chicken cooked through.

3 Meanwhile cook the rice using your preferred method as described in the introduction on page 70.

4 Stir the prawns, coriander and a few shakes of Tabasco into the gumbo and simmer gently for 3 minutes. Spoon the rice into two serving bowls and top with gumbo. Serve hot.

JAMBALAYA • CAJUN GUMBO

RISI E BISI

REALLY EASY!

Risi e Bisi is a thick, soupy rice dish that is a speciality of Venice – it simply means rice and peas. Vegetarians can leave out the bacon.

Serves 2
knob of butter
small onion, chopped
2 garlic cloves, finely chopped
3 rashers streaky bacon, chopped
125g (4 oz) risotto rice
750 ml (1¼ pints) chicken or vegetable stock
250g (8 oz) frozen peas
1 tablespoon chopped fresh parsley
1 tablespoon freshly grated Parmesan
salt and freshly ground black pepper

1 Heat the butter in a large saucepan and gently cook the onion, garlic and bacon for 5 minutes until softened.

2 Add the rice and cook for a minute. Pour over the stock, stir well and bring to the boil. Cover and simmer, stirring occasionally for 15 minutes. If it becomes too dry, add a little more stock.

3 Stir in the peas and cook for 4 minutes. Stir in the parsley, Parmesan and season well to taste. Divide into soup bowls and serve with warm crusty bread.

WARM BULGUR WHEAT SALAD

REALLY EASY!

Add variety to this simple supper dish by serving the grilled vegetables on a bed of rice or couscous in place of the bulgur wheat.

Serves 2

300 ml (½ pint) vegetable stock
125g (4 oz) bulgur wheat
1 courgette, sliced lengthways
1 small aubergine, sliced lengthways
1 red pepper, cut into 8 strips, lengthways
125g (4 oz) large mushrooms, thickly sliced
1 tablespoon olive oil

For The Dressing

2 tablespoons olive oil
juice of half a lemon
1 garlic clove, finely chopped
1 tablespoon chopped fresh parsley
pinch of sugar
seasoning

1 Place the stock in a saucepan and bring to the boil. Tip in the bulgur wheat, turn off the heat and cover with a lid. Leave the grains for 20 minutes to absorb the water and puff up while you grill the vegetables.

2 Arrange the vegetables in the grill pan and brush with the tablespoon of olive oil. Sprinkle lightly with salt and grill for about 8 minutes on each side until tender and golden.

3 Meanwhile make the dressing by whisking all the ingredients together with a fork. Spoon the warm bulgur wheat onto two plates and arrange the grilled vegetables on top. Drizzle over the dressing and serve immediately

RISI E BISI • WARM BULGAR WHEAT SALAD

BREAD & FLOUR

There's nothing in the world more appetising than the smell of freshly baking bread. When you walk into a supermarket that has an in-store bakery, you will always catch the smell of the bread. I'm not sure if they plan it purposefully as the bakery always seems to be at the other side of the shop, but it certainly sets your tummy rumbling and your hand reaching out for a currant bun.

INTRODUCTION

The range of breads now readily available is quite incredible. It is easy to buy freshly baked bread in all shapes, sizes, textures and flavours, from Italian olive breads to Greek pittas and Irish soda bread. With such a choice, there's no reason why bread shouldn't be a fundamental part of your diet.

STORING BREAD

If you buy your bread fresh from a bakery, it is best eaten the day you buy it but it will last a couple of days if you store it in a cool, dry cupboard in its paper wrapper to allow the bread to breathe. If it goes hard the next day, pop into a hot oven for 5 minutes to heat through and soften. If you buy sliced, plastic wrapped bread, you can store it for longer because of the additives used in large scale bread production, but it will go mouldy rather than hard after a few days. If you can't eat a whole loaf within a week, keep it in the freezer and pull out slices as you need them.

FLOUR

Even if you're not a baker, you should always make sure you have a small packet of plain flour in your cupboard. Use it to thicken soups and sauces, coat meat and vegetables for frying as in the courgette wheels (page 154) and barbecued spare ribs (page 140), to roll out ready-made pastry, make dumplings (page 102) and batters for pancakes (page 108) and toad in the hole (page 101). And if you can remember learning to make puff pastry at school, you will be able to appreciate why ready-made pastry is such a blessing. It can be bought both fresh and frozen and you will only need to use half a packet to make enough for two, and the remainder can be kept covered in the fridge for a couple of days.

CHEESY BREAD AND BUTTER PUDDING

REALLY EASY!

A delicious savoury version of bread and butter pudding.

Serves 2
6 slices white bread, crusts removed
large knob of butter or margarine
180g (6 oz) Cheddar, or other cheese, grated
1 small onion, finely chopped
1 tablespoon chopped fresh parsley
1 large egg
300 ml (½ pint) milk
seasoning

1 Preheat the oven to 180C,350F,Gas 4. Spread the butter on the bread and cut each slice into four triangles. Butter an ovenproof dish and arrange the bread in the dish sprinkling with cheese, onion, parsley and a little seasoning between each layer.

2 Beat together the milk and egg and season lightly. Pour the liquid over the layers and bake in the oven for 30 minutes until well risen and golden.

BASIC PIZZA DOUGH

EASY!

Makes 4 individual pizzas
400g (14 oz) plain flour
2 teaspoons easy-blend dried yeast
1 teaspoon salt
2 tablespoons olive oil
250 ml (8 fl oz)warm water

1 Place the flour, yeast and salt in a large bowl. Make a well in the centre and pour in the water. Using your hand to mix, bring the ingredients together to form a soft, pliable dough. Turn the dough out onto a lightly floured work surface and knead vigorously for at least 5 minutes until the dough is smooth and stretchy. Because all flours are slightly different, you may find that you need to add extra flour or water to get a good, soft but not too sticky dough.

2 Rub a little oil over the surface of the ball of dough, put into a large bowl and cover with a clean tea towel and leave in a warm place for about 30 minutes until doubled in size. Divide the dough into four equal balls and knead them again for a couple of minutes. Roll out the dough to the size and thickness you like, remembering that it will be at least double in thickness by the time it is cooked, and place on baking sheets.

3 Preheat the oven to 240C,475F,Gas 9. Arrange the toppings on your pizzas, except the cheese, if using and place in the oven for 10 minutes. Sprinkle over the cheese and return to the oven for a further 5-10 minutes until the pizza is crisp and golden brown.

PIZZA TOPPINGS

The quickest and one of the best sauces to use as a base for pizza is passata. This can be bought from most supermarkets in a carton or bottle and is made from sieved plum tomatoes. Spread it over the dough, sprinkle with a little good olive oil and season lightly with salt, pepper and some dried oregano or basil before adding your choice of toppings. The quantities given are for each individual pizza.

MARINARA THE ORIGINAL PIZZA
2-3 tablespoons passata, pinch dried oregano, 1 finely chopped garlic clove, 1 teaspoon olive oil, seasoning.

NEOPOLITANA
2-3 tablespoons passata, 2 canned anchovy fillets, 6 pickled capers, 4 black olives, 1 teaspoon olive oil, 30g (1 oz) chopped mozzarella cheese, seasoning.

PESCATORA
2-3 tablespoons passata, pinch dried basil, 60g (2 oz) ready-prepared seafood cocktail, thawed if frozen, 1 finely chopped garlic clove, 1 teaspoon olive oil, seasoning.

FUNGHI
2-3 tablespoons passata, pinch dried oregano, 60g (2 oz) sliced mushrooms, 1 chopped garlic clove, 30g (1 oz) chopped mozzarella cheese, 1 teaspoon olive oil, seasoning.

BASIC PIZZA DOUGH • PIZZA TOPPINGS

99

TABLE TOP NAAN

EASY!

Definitely the most fashionable food to be seen eating is a balti curry which has to be served with the compulsory table-top naan. Impress your friends with your own, home-made bumper naan breads.

Serves 2

250g (8 oz) self raising flour
3 tablespoons live natural yogurt
1 teaspoon easy-blend dried yeast
1 teaspoon salt
small knob of butter

1 Place the flour, yeast and salt together in a large bowl and make a well in the centre. Spoon in the yogurt and gradually add about 6 tablespoons of warm water, bringing the mixture together to form a very soft, slightly sticky dough. Knead lightly for 1 minute then cover with a tea-towel and leave in a warm place for about an hour.

2 Preheat the grill to high. Divide the dough into 2 equal pieces and roll out on a lightly floured surface into two large rectangles, each as big as your grill pan. Place under the grill for about 1 minute on the first side and 30 seconds on the other, until puffed and lightly browned. When the naans are ready, and still hot, spread them with a little butter.

TOAD IN THE HOLE

EASY!

Toad in the hole doesn't usually have onions it, but I think they add flavour and texture to the dish. If you're a traditionalist, leave them out. It is important to heat a little oil in the baking dish before you pour in the batter as it creates a seal and prevents sticking.

Serves 2

60g (2 oz) flour
1 egg, beaten
150 ml (¼ pint) milk
2 tablespoons vegetable oil
1 onion, thinly sliced into rings
250g (8 oz) pork sausages
seasoning

1 Preheat the oven to 200C, 400F, Gas 6. Sift the flour into a bowl with a little salt and pepper. Make a well in the centre and pour in the egg and half the milk. Beat to make a stiff batter and gradually work in the remaining milk. Set aside to rest for a few minutes while you fry the sausages.

2 Heat 1 tablespoon oil in a large frying pan and cook the sausages and onion rings for 10 minutes until golden. Remove and drain. Place remaining tablespoon of oil in a shallow, heat proof dish and place in the oven for a few minutes. Remove the dish from the oven and put in the sausages and onions. Pour over the batter and bake for 30 minutes until the batter has risen and is crisp and golden.

BEEF STEW AND DUMPLINGS

REALLY EASY!

Although beef stew takes quite a long time, it is very easy and cheap to make, and you can leave the pot simmering away whilst you get on with some revision. Use any root vegetables you fancy for this dish, try parsnips or turnips. I have specified vegetable suet as it is a less-saturated fat than the original animal suet, but both types produce an equally good dumpling.

Serves 2-3

500g (1 lb) stewing steak, cubed
2 tablespoons flour
1 tablespoon vegetable oil
1 large onion, sliced
900 ml (1½ pints) beef stock
1 large potato, cubed
2 large carrots, thickly sliced

For The Dumplings

125g (4 oz) self raising flour
1 teaspoon dried parsley
60g (2 oz) vegetable suet
seasoning

1 Season the flour and place in a small polythene bag, toss in the meat and shake the bag until the meat is evenly coated.

2 Heat the oil in a large saucepan and fry the beef and onion for 5 minutes until browned. Pour over the stock, cover and simmer for 1 hour.

3 Add the vegetables to the beef and simmer for 10 minutes whilst you make the dumplings. Place the flour, parsley, suet and a pinch of salt in a bowl. Add about 4 tablespoons of warm water and mix together to make a soft dough.

4 Shape into 6 small balls and drop into the stew. Cover and cook for 15-20 minutes until meat, dumplings and vegetables are tender. Season to taste and serve.

BEEF STEW & DUMPLINGS

QUICK COURGETTE AND LEEK PUFF TART

EASY!

A crisp puff pastry case containing leeks, onoin, courgettes and anchovies.

Serves 2

knob of butter or margarine
1 large leek, sliced
1 onion, sliced
2 courgettes, sliced
can of anchovies in olive oil
250g (8 oz) ready made puff pastry, thawed if frozen
freshly ground black pepper

1 Preheat the oven to 220C,425F,Gas 7. Melt the butter in a large frying pan and add the leek, onion and courgette. Tear each anchovy in half and add to the pan with the oil from the can. Cook gently for about 10 minutes, until softened. Season well with black pepper.

2 Meanwhile, roll the pastry out into a large rectangle, about 1 cm (½ inch) thick. Using a small sharp knife, cut a border about ½ cm (¼ inch) wide inside the rectangle – cut deep into the pastry, but not right through.

3 Spread the courgette mixture onto the pastry, but within the border. Transfer to a baking sheet and place in the oven for 15-20 minutes until the border has risen up to provide a puffy golden rim to the tart. Serve hot or at room temperature with a crisp green salad.

CHEESE AND HAM PASTIES

Why not make double the recipe – these little pasties are good for a packed lunch.

Serves 2
250g (8 oz) ready made puff pastry, thawed if frozen
180g (6 oz) Cheddar or similar cheese, grated
60g (2 oz) wafer thin ham
1 tablespoon chopped fresh parsley or chives
1 egg
2 tablespoons milk
seasoning

1 Preheat the oven to 220C, 425F, Gas 7. Roll the pastry out into a large rectangle, measuring 30 cm x 15 cm (12 inch x 6 inch). Cut in half to give two 15 cm (6 inch) squares.

2 Sprinkle the cheese on one half of each square and season well. Top with the chopped herbs and the ham. Beat together the egg and milk and brush a little around the edges. Fold over to make a triangle and press down well along the edges to seal.

3 Transfer to a baking sheet and brush all over with the egg. Place in the oven for 15-20 minutes until puffed and golden. Serve with salad or vegetables.

QUICK COURGETTE & LEEK PUFF TART • CHEESE & HAM PASTIES

CREAMY VEGETABLE COBBLER

 A mixture of broccli, leek and peas in a cheese sauce, topped with a light scone mixture.

Serves 2
1 tablespoon vegetable oil
1 garlic clove, finely chopped
250g (8 oz) broccoli, cut into florets
1 large leek, thickly sliced
250g (8 oz) frozen peas, thawed
30g (1 oz) butter or margarine
30g (1 oz) flour
300 ml (½ pint) milk
125g (4 oz) Cheddar cheese, grated

For The Cobbler Topping
125g (4 oz) self raising flour
60g (2 oz) butter or margarine, cut into small pieces
2 tablespoons milk
1 tablespoon chopped fresh parsley or 1 teaspoon dried
seasoning

1 Preheat the oven to 220C,425F,Gas 7. Heat the oil in a large saucepan and gently fry garlic, broccoli, leek and peas for 8 minutes until softened. Transfer the vegetables to a deep casserole dish.

2 Heat the butter in the same pan, stir in the flour and cook for 1 minute. Gradually add the milk, stirring until thickened. Bring to the boil and simmer gently for 3 minutes. Add all but a handful of the grated cheese, and stir until melted. Season to taste and pour over the vegetables.

3 Season the flour well with salt and pepper and then using just your fingertips, rub the butter into the flour until it resembles breadcrumbs. Stir in the parsley and milk and bring the mixture together to make a firm dough – add a little more milk if it feels too dry.

4 Shape the mixture into 8 balls and flatten each one gently with the palm of your hand. Arrange them on top of the casserole and sprinkle over the reserved cheese. Bake for 20 minutes until the cobbler topping is risen and golden.

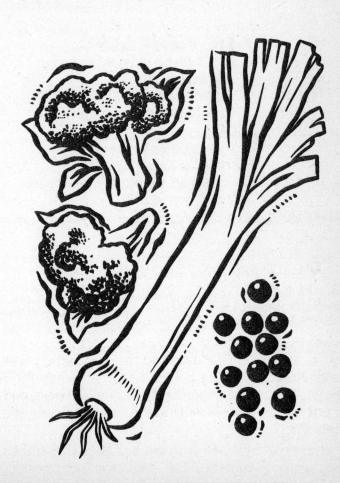

PANCAKES

EASY!

**Pancakes are a fantastic base for lots of
different meals. They are used extensively in
Mexican, Chinese and French cooking as well as
English. Why wait until Pancake day, try cooking
some of the following recipes next time you're
stuck for ideas.**

BASIC PANCAKES

Makes 8

125g (4 oz) flour
¼ teaspoon of salt
300 ml (½ pint) milk
1 egg, beaten
small knob of butter, melted
vegetable oil, for frying

1 Sieve the flour and salt into a bowl and make a well in
the centre.

2 Add the egg and milk and whisk vigorously to make a
smooth batter. Beat in the melted butter.

3 Heat a little oil in a small, shallow non-stick frying pan.
Spoon in 2 tablespoons of mixture and swirl to cover the
base of the pan. Cook for a few seconds, flip over and
cook the second side. Repeat to make 8 pancakes in total.

STUFFING SUGGESTIONS

Try adding chopped herbs to the basic batter, cook and fill with one of the suggestions below. Roll up, sprinkle over a little grated cheese and heat through under the grill.

Chilli Con Carne (page 119)

Garlic Mushrooms (page 141)

Curried Beans (page 124)

Ratatouille (page 131)

Guacamole (page 146) **and Sour Cream**

SWEET IDEAS

Sprinkle hot pancakes with a little caster sugar and top with one of the following:

Toasted marshmallows with melted chocolate

Mashed banana and Greek-style yogurt

Canned mandarin segments with condensed milk

Grilled peach slices with honey and flaked almonds

A squeeze of orange or lemon juice

FILO PARCELS WITH FETA AND SPINACH

Filo pastry is very delicate and can crack easily if allowed to dry out. Dust lightly with flour and loosely cover with cling film when it's waiting to be used.

Serves 2

1 tablespoon olive oil
1 garlic clove, sliced
250g (8 oz) fresh spinach or 180g (6 oz) frozen leaf spinach, thawed
2 tomatoes, chopped
seasoning
30g (1 oz) butter, melted
4 large sheets filo pastry
125g (4 oz) feta cheese, crumbled
1 teaspoon cornflour
1 tablespoon water

1 Preheat the oven to 190C,375F,Gas 5. Heat the olive oil in a large frying pan and cook the garlic, spinach and tomatoes together over a fairly high heat for 5 minutes. Season to taste, strain in a sieve, reserving the juices and leave for 10 minutes to cool.

2 Brush two sheets of pastry with some of the melted butter and place one on top of the other, buttered side uppermost. Cut in half lengthways to give two strips. Place a quarter of the spinach mixture in one corner of each pastry strip and crumble the feta cheese on top.

3 Fold the pastry and filling over at right angles to make a triangle and continue folding in this way along the strip of pastry to form a neat triangular parcel. Repeat with the remaining pastry and mixture to make four even-sized parcels.

4 Place on a baking sheet and brush with remaining melted butter and bake for 20 minutes until golden and crisp. Meanwhile, blend the cornflour with a tablespoon of water and stir into the reserved juices. Bring to the boil and simmer gently for 2 minutes. Serve the parcels with mashed potato and sauce.

FILO PARCELS WITH FETA & SPINACH

SAUCY STIR-FRY ON TOAST

REALLY EASY

A strange sounding name for a fabulously, warming dish that takes just a few minutes to prepare.

Serves 2
1 large potato, peeled and cubed
1 tablespoon vegetable oil
2 bacon rashers, roughly chopped (optional)
2 leeks, sliced
1 apple, cubed
3 leaves Savoy cabbage, shredded
2 tablespoon soy sauce
2 large, thick slices of hot buttered toast
seasoning

1 Par-cook the potatoes in boiling, salted water for 5 minutes.

2 Meanwhile, stir-fry the the bacon and leeks for 3 minutes, add the drained potato cubes and continue to cook for 5 minutes. Add the apple, cabbage, soy sauce and about 5 tablespoons of water and cook for a further 5 minutes.

3 Pile on top of the hot buttered toast and serve immediately.

HOT TOMATO BAGUETTE

R E A L L Y   E A S Y

 Try topping these with some grated mozzarella or thin slices of onion or courgette.

Serves 2
1 French stick
2 tablespoons pesto sauce
4 large tomatoes, sliced
1 tablespoon olive oil
1 garlic clove, finely chopped
1 tablespoon freshly grated Parmesan
seasoning

1 Preheat the oven to 200C, 400F, Gas 6. Split the French stick in half lengthways. Spread thinly with pesto sauce and arrange the tomato slices on top.

2 Brush the tomatoes with olive oil and sprinkle with garlic, seasoning and Parmesan. Bake directly on the oven shelf for about 8 minutes until hot and crunchy.

SAUCY STIR-FRY ON TOAST • HOT TOMATO BAGUETTE

CHEESY KIPPER TOASTS

REALLY EASY

Boil-in-the-bag kippers are a great invention - it means that you can eat kippers whenever you want without them leaving their odour on your grill pan for weeks. If you like, try this recipe with peppered mackerel fillets.

Serves 2
1 pack boil in the bag kippers
60g (2 oz) Cheddar, grated
3 tablespoons Greek yogurt
1 teaspoon Worcestershire sauce
2 large, thick slices of hot buttered toast
black pepper

1 Cook the kippers according to packet instructions. Mash well with a fork and mix in the cheese, yogurt and Worcestershire sauce.

2 Spread the mixture onto the toast and sprinkle generously with black pepper. Place under a hot grill for 3-4 minutes until bubbling and golden. Eat straight away.

VEGETABLES
& BEANS

This food group is immense, with shapes, colours, sizes and flavours stretching across the whole spectrum. You are sure to see different, odd-looking vegetables when you go to the shops, as the range of imported goods becomes wider and more varied each day. Once you've mastered home-grown produce, you might like to start experimenting with dishes that involve something more exotic, but for the moment stick to what you know.

INTRODUCTION

EAT SEASONALLY

It makes sense to base your meals around what is in season. Fresh fruit and vegetables in the peak of their season have far more flavour than those imported from hotter climates or grown in greenhouses to meet out of season demand. Not only do seasonal vegetables taste better, they're also a lot cheaper.

Here's a quick guide to when fruits and vegetables are at their seasonal best, and cheapest to buy.

January	avocados, sweet potatoes
February	lemons, limes, pink grapefruit, marrows
March	broccoli, white cabbage, spring greens
April	cauliflower, mushrooms, leaks
May	new potatoes, asparagus, spinach, rhubarb, cucumber
June	courgettes, peas, mangetout, salad lettuces, broad beans, strawberries, watercress, radishes
July	peppers, runner beans, globe artichokes, currants, peaches, nectarines
August	corn on the cob, celery, pak choi, aubergines, blackberries, apricots
September	marrows and squashes, plums

October	red cabbage, parsnips, swedes, potatoes, turnips, pumpkins, apples, pears
November	leeks, shallots, Brussels' sprouts, oranges
December	beetroot, cabbages (red & white) Jerusalem artichokes, nuts, figs

SHOPPING

Buy fresh fruit and vegetables from your local market, if you can, because the prices will be substantially lower than in the supermarket or corner shop, and if you shop on the way home from college, you're sure to pick up some end-of-day bargains. As mentioned in the Eating Well chapter, it is best not to store fresh vegetables for too long so don't buy in bulk. If you only need two carrots, don't feel you have to buy a whole pound.

BEANS

It is very cheap and easy to buy dried beans and soak and cook them yourself, but it means you have to plan your meal at least a day in advance. There is such an excellent array of inexpensive canned beans on the shelves of supermarkets, that I'm not sure how many people actually take the time to cook dried beans. But for those of you who do want to, it is very important that you follow this guide carefully, as certain beans, particularly kidney beans, contain toxins that can make you quite ill if they are not destroyed by cooking:

TO COOK DRIED BEANS

1 Place the beans in a sieve or colander and rinse well, remove any pieces of grit. Tip into a large bowl, fill with cold water and leave for 8 hours, or overnight, to soak. Don't soak for over 24 hours or the beans will start to ferment.

2 Rinse well and place in a large saucepan. Cover with cold water, bring to the boil and boil rapidly for 15 minutes.

3 Drain and rinse well. Place in a saucepan and cover with clean cold water, bring to the boil and simmer, uncovered for 1-1½ hours until tender. Don't add salt as it can toughen the beans.

CHILLI CON CARNE

REALLY EASY!

A hot spicy mixture of beef, chillies, tomatoes and kidney beans.

Serves 2-3

1 tablespoon vegetable oil
1 onion, chopped
1 garlic clove, finely chopped
1 fresh chilli, finely chopped
250g (8 oz) lean minced beef
400g (14 oz) can chopped tomatoes
400g (14 oz) can red kidney beans, drained
2 teaspoons hot chilli powder
seasoning

1 Heat the oil in a large frying pan and cook the onion, garlic, chilli and mince for 5 minutes until the vegetables are softened and the meat is no longer pink.

2 Stir in the tomatoes, kidney beans, chilli powder and a little seasoning. Cover and simmer for 45 minutes.

3 Serve with ready-made tacos or boiled rice.

ZESTY LENTIL SOUP

REALLY EASY!

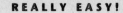

V **Lentils are a brilliant ingredient to keep close at hand. They don't need soaking, they're very nutritious and make the best soups and curries.**

Serves 2
1 celery stick, chopped
1 carrot, chopped
1 small onion, chopped
1 garlic clove, chopped
1 cm (½ inch) piece fresh ginger, grated
1 teaspoon cumin seeds
60g (2 oz) red lentils
900 ml (1½ pints) vegetable stock
grated rind and juice of a lime
seasoning

1 Heat the oil in a large saucepan and fry the celery, carrot, onion, garlic, ginger and cumin seeds for 5 minutes.

2 Add the lentils and stock, bring to the boil, cover and simmer for 30 minutes.

3 Stir in the lime juice and grated rind and season to taste. Serve with warm crusty bread.

THAI CHICKPEA CURRY

REALLY EASY!

Chickpeas are often used as the base of Thai curries, and with the addition of typical flavourings, coriander and coconut, this recipe gives an aromatic, sophisticated-tasting curry that's actually very easy to make

Serves 2
2 garlic cloves
handful of fresh coriander
1 small green chilli, seeded
1 tablespoon vegetable oil
2 potatoes, cut into small dice
400g (14 oz) can chickpeas, drained
2 tomatoes, cut into wedges
300 ml (½ pint) coconut milk
1 tablespoon soy sauce
pinch of sugar
seasoning

1 Use a heavy knife to chop together the garlic, chilli and coriander until blended into a paste.

2 Heat the oil in a large saucepan and fry the paste for a minute. Toss in the potato, chickpeas, tomatoes and coconut milk, cover with a lid and simmer for 15 minutes until the potatoes are tender.

3 Season to taste with the soy sauce, sugar, salt. and pepper. Serve with rice or noodles.

SPINACH AND CANNELLINI BEAN STEW

EASY!

This is one of those dishes that tastes even better the next day, it just needs a quick warm through in a saucepan. If you can't get hold of fresh spinach, use frozen leaf spinach instead.

Serves 2
1 tablespoon olive oil, plus extra for serving
2 rashers of streaky bacon, chopped (optional)
1 onion, chopped
1 garlic clove, finely chopped
1 very large potato, cut into chunks
1.2 litres (2 pints) vegetable or chicken stock
250g (8 oz) fresh leaf spinach
400g (14 oz) can cannellini beans, drained
salt and freshly ground black pepper

1 Heat the oil in a large saucepan and cook the bacon, onion and garlic for 2 minutes. Add the potato and stir-fry for a further 3 minutes.

2 Pour in the stock, bring to the boil and simmer, uncovered for 30 minutes. Add the spinach and cannellini beans and cook for 10 minutes.

3 Season to taste and divide between two bowls. Swirl a little olive oil into each bowl and sprinkleover some black pepper.

FALAFEL

E A S Y !

V Give refectory food a miss and pack some falafel in pitta pockets for your lunch. Or eat with Greek salad for a satisfying supper.

Serves 2-4
400g (14 oz) can chickpeas, drained
half a small onion, very finely chopped
1 hot red chilli, very finely chopped
¼ teaspoon ground cumin
1 tablespoon chopped fresh coriander
1 egg, lightly beaten
2 tablespoons flour
vegetable oil for frying
seasoning

1 Mash the chickpeas, onion, chilli, cumin and coriander well together and season to taste. It may take a while to get the mixture soft enough to shape, as chickpeas can be quite dry and firm, but persevere and the mixture should come together.

2 Shape into 8 round balls and flatten into patties. Dip first into the beaten egg and then into the flour, shaking off any excess. Heat the oil in a frying pan and cook the patties for 2-3 minutes until golden brown. Drain well on kitchen paper.

SPINACH & CANNELLINI BEAN STEW • FALAFEL

CURRIED BEANS

REALLY EASY!

 **This is a wonderfully colourful and fragrant dish.
Serve with mashed or baked potatoes.**

Serves 2
2 tablespoons vegetable oil
1 onion, finely chopped
2 garlic cloves, finely chopped
1 cm (½ inch) piece fresh ginger, finely grated
2 tablespoons hot curry paste
400g (14 oz) can haricot or cannellini beans, drained
400g (14 oz) can chopped tomatoes
60g (2 oz) raisins
1 apple, peeled and diced
seasoning

1 Heat the oil in a large saucepan and cook the onion, garlic and ginger for 5 minutes until softened. Add the curry paste and stir-fry for 2 minutes.

2 Stir in the beans, tomatoes, raisins and apple and season well to taste. Gently simmer together for 20 minutes.

(35)

(V)

CARROT AND ORANGE SOUP

REALLY EASY!

This is an unbelievably easy, but tasty soup that can happily be reheated the next day. It's fat free, so it's perfect for anyone counting their calories. Serve with hot buttered toast.

Serves 2
600 ml (1 pint) vegetable stock
2 large carrots, grated
1 small onion, finely chopped
1 garlic clove, finely chopped
1 small potato, grated
juice of 2 oranges
1 tablespoon chopped fresh coriander or parsley
seasoning

1 Place the stock, carrot, onion, garlic and potato together in a large saucepan. Bring to the boil, cover and simmer for 20 minutes.

2 Stir in the orange juice and herbs and season to taste. Heat through and simmer for 5 minutes. Serve as it is, or if you prefer, liquidise, or pass through a metal sieve for a smoother, thicker soup.

CURRIED BEANS • CARROT & ORANGE SOUP

MUSHROOM SOUP WITH GARLIC CROUTONS

EASY!

A creamy mushroom soup served with crunchy croutons which makes a filling supper dish.

Serves 2
knob of margarine or butter
2 garlic cloves, finely chopped
4 spring onions, finely sliced
2 tablespoons plain flour
600 ml (1 pint) hot vegetable stock
250g (8 oz) mushrooms, finely chopped
150 ml (¼ pint) single cream
seasoning

For The Croutons
2 tablespoons olive oil
1 large garlic clove, quartered
1 thick slice of bread, cubed

1 Melt the margarine in a large saucepan and gently cook the garlic and spring onions for 3 minutes until softened. Add the flour and stir for 1 minute. Gradually beat in the stock. Bring to the boil, add the mushrooms, cover and simmer for 30 minutes.

2 Meanwhile, heat the oil in a small frying pan and cook the garlic for 5 minutes until golden, take care not to burn it. Remove and discard the oil, toss in the bread and stir fry for 2-3 minutes until golden. Drain on kitchen paper.

3 Stir the cream into the soup and season to taste. Heat through gently, pour into bowls and sprinkle with the croutons.

STUFFED PEPPERS

EASY!

Red peppers, stuffed with raisins, mushrooms, tomatoes, parsley and garlic, and baked in the oven.

Serves 2

125g (4 oz) long grain rice
2 red peppers
2 tablespoons raisins
6 button mushrooms, sliced
2 tomatoes, diced
2 tablespoons chopped fresh parsley
2 garlic cloves, finely chopped
2 tablespoons white wine vinegar
1 tablespoon clear honey
3 tablespoons olive oil
seasoning

1 Wash the rice well and cook in boiling water for 15-20 minutes until tender. Drain well and set aside to cool.

2 Preheat the oven to 200C,400F,Gas 6. Twist the stalks out of the peppers, turn them upside down and tap the bottom to shake out all the seeds.

3 Place the raisins, mushrooms, tomatoes, parsley, garlic, vinegar, honey and 2 tablespoons of olive oil in a large bowl. Add the rice, mix well together, and season to taste.

4 Spoon the mixture into the peppers, pressing down with the back of the spoon. Carefully lie the peppers down in a small roasting tin, brush with the remaining oil, cover with foil and bake for 40 minutes until tender.

MUSHROOM SOUP WITH GARLIC CRUTONS • STUFFED PEPPERS

STUFFED AUBERGINES

EASY!

This dish cannot be prepared in advance, but once cooked can be covered and kept in the fridge for a couple of days and served cold with a crisp salad.

Serves 2
1 large aubergine
2 slices of white bread, grated into crumbs
1 egg, beaten
60g (2 oz) mozzarella or Cheddar cheese, cut into small dice
2 tablespoons chopped fresh parsley
2 garlic cloves, finely sliced
2 large tomatoes, sliced
½ teaspoon dried oregano
seasoning

1 Preheat the oven to 200C,400F,Gas 6. Cut the aubergine in half lengthwise and using a tablespoon, scoop out the flesh to leave a ½ cm (¼ inch) thick shell.

2 Finely chop the flesh with a heavy knife and place in a bowl with the breadcrumbs, egg, cheese, parsley and garlic. Season well and mix together.

3 Pile back into the shells, pressing down with the back of the spoon. Arrange the tomato layers on top and sprinkle with the dried oregano and little freshly ground black pepper.

4 Pour 4 tablespoons of water into a small roasting tin and carefully stand the aubergine halves in the water. Bake for 30-40 minutes until tender and browned on top.

HUMMUS

REALLY EASY!

Tahini is sesame seed paste and can be bought in health food shops and selected supermarkets, if you prefer, you could use smooth peanut butter in its place. Hummus will keep covered in the fridge for a few days and is delicious spread thickly on hot buttered toast.

400g (14 oz) can chickpeas, drained
2 garlic cloves, crushed
6 tablespoons olive oil
4 tablespoons tahini
juice of a lemon
seasoning

1 Mash together the chickpeas and garlic until fairly smooth. Gradually beat in the olive oil to give a creamy consistency.

2 Stir in the tahini, lemon juice and seasoning , adding more, or less, than the given amounts, to suit your taste.

STUFFED AUBERGINES • HUMMUS

PINEAPPLE AND BEANSPROUT STIR-FRY

REALLY EASY!

Serve this stir fry with boiled rice or egg noodles.

Serves 2
1 tablespoon vegetable oil
1 onion, thinly sliced
2.5 cm (1 inch) piece fresh ginger, grated
250g (8 oz) can pineapple chunks in natural juice
180g (6 oz) button mushrooms, halved
½ teaspoon five spice powder
1 tablespoon soy sauce
1 tablespoon vinegar
250g (8 oz) fresh beansprouts
seasoning

1 Heat the oil in a wok or large frying pan until very hot, and quickly fry the onion and ginger for 2 minutes. Toss in the pineapple chunks and juice, button mushrooms and five spice powder and stir-fry for 5 minutes.

2 Flavour with soy sauce and vinegar, toss in the beansprouts and cook for a further 3 minutes until the beansprouts have just wilted. Check the seasoning and serve immediately.

RATATOUILLE

REALLY EASY!

V **Any leftover ratatouille can be mixed with a little French dressing and served cold as salad.**

Serves 2
2 tablespoons olive oil
1 large onion, chopped
2 garlic cloves, finely chopped
250g (8 oz) ripe tomatoes, roughly chopped
1 small aubergine, diced
2 courgettes, thickly sliced
1 red pepper, diced
2 tablespoons chopped fresh basil or 1 teaspoon dried
pinch of sugar
1 tablespoon tomato purée
seasoning

1 Heat the oil in a large saucepan and cook the onion and garlic for 5 minutes until softened. Add the tomatoes and cook for a further 2 minutes.

2 Stir in the aubergine, pepper, courgette, basil, sugar and purée. Cover and simmer gently for 30 minutes. Season to taste and serve.

PINEAPPLE & BEANSPROUT STIR-FRY • RATATOUILLE

SPICY BEAN BURGERS

E A S Y !

 Burgers made with butterbeans and spinach and flavoured with garlic, chilli, cumin and coriander.

Serves 2
1 tablespoon vegetable oil
1 small onion, finely chopped
2 garlic cloves, finely chopped
1 small hot red chilli, finely chopped
400g (14 oz) can butterbeans
125g (4 oz) frozen chopped spinach, thawed
60g (2 oz) fresh breadcrumbs
1 teaspoon ground cumin
1 tablespoon chopped fresh coriander
seasoning

1 Heat the oil in a small saucepan and fry the onion, garlic and chilli for 5 minutes until softened.

2 Mash the beans well and place in a bowl with the spinach, breadcrumbs, cumin and coriander. Add the fried onion mixture and stir well together.

3 Season to taste and shape into four round burgers. Grill or shallow fry for a few minutes on each side until crisp and golden. Serve in burger buns with relish and salad.

TUNA AND BEAN SALAD

REALLY EASY!

**Layers of beans, cucumber, tomatoes, onions
and tuna, moistened with a garlic lemon dressing**

Serves 2

*400g (14 oz) can mixed beans, drained
half a cucumber, diced
2 tomatoes, diced
1 tablespoon chopped fresh parsley
1 red onion, thinly sliced into rings
180g (6 oz) can tuna in oil, drained
2 tablespoons olive oil
juice of half a lemon
1 garlic clove, crushed
seasoning*

1 Place the beans, cucumber, tomatoes and parsley in a
bowl and mix well together. Transfer to a serving plate.

2 Arrange onion rings and chunks of tuna on top of the
beans. Whisk together the olive oil, lemon juice, garlic
and plenty of seasoning. Drizzle over the salad and serve
immediately.

SPICY BEAN BURGERS • TUNA & BEAN SALAD

CASSOULET

EASY

A cassoulet is a French bean stew that's topped with breadcrumbs and finished in the oven. Try this recipe with any type of beans.

Serves 2
2 tablespoons vegetable oil
1 onion, sliced
2 garlic cloves, chopped
1 celery stick, chopped
400g (14 oz) can mixed beans, drained
200g (7 oz) can chopped tomatoes
½ teaspoon dried mixed herbs
2 pork chops
60g (2 oz) fresh breadcrumbs
seasoning

1 Preheat the oven to 190C,375F,Gas 5. Heat one tablespoon of vegetable oil in a large saucepan and gently cook the onion, garlic and celery for 5 minutes until softened. Add the beans, tomatoes, herbs and 150 ml (¼ pint) of water. Season to taste and simmer together for 10 minutes.

2 Meanwhile, fry the the pork chops for 3-4 minutes on each side until lightly browned. Transfer half the bean mixture into a casserole dish and place the chops on top. Spoon over the remaining bean mixture.

3 Sprinkle over the breadcrumbs and bake for 40 minutes until golden.

ORIENTAL PRAWN STIR-FRY

REALLY EASY

Fresh ginger can be bought in most supermarkets, just snap off a small piece and it will only cost a few pence.

Serves 2
2 tablespoons vegetable oil
2 garlic cloves, chopped
1 cm (½ inch) piece fresh ginger, peeled and finely chopped
125g (4 oz) button mushrooms, sliced
125g (4 oz) broccoli florets
60g (2 oz) frozen peas
125g (4 oz) large peeled prawns
2 tablespoons soy sauce
1 tablespoon sesame seeds
seasoning

1 Heat the oil in a wok and quickly stir-fry the garlic and ginger for 2 minutes. Add the vegetables and prawns and cook for a further 5 minutes.

2 Add the soy sauce and 2 tablespoons of water and season to taste. Sprinkle in the sesame seeds and cook for 2 minutes until the vegetables are just tender and the stir-fry is piping hot. Serve with boiled rice or noodles.

CASSOULET • ORIENTAL PRAWN STIR-FRY

MIXED VEGETABLE GRATIN

REALLY EASY!

Large flat mushrooms give lots of flavour to this tasty dish of vegetables topped with grilled cheese.

Serves 2

2 tablespoons olive oil
2 courgettes, thickly sliced
4 large flat mushrooms, thickly sliced
2 large tomatoes, thickly sliced
½ teaspoon dried oregano
60g (2 oz) Cheddar, grated
seasoning

1 Heat the oil in a large frying pan and cook the mushrooms and courgettes for about 5 minutes until softened. Add the tomatoes and cook for a further 5 minutes and season to taste.

2 Transfer the vegetables to a heatproof dish and sprinkle over the cheese. Place under a preheated grill for 5 minutes until bubbling and golden. Serve immediately with salad and bread.

SALAD NICOISE

R E A L L Y   E A S Y !

Salad Niçoise is an essential summertime recipe. It can be made a number of ways but generally contains hard boiled eggs, anchovies and black olives. Serve with a French stick, some sparkling mineral water, and you'll have a fine feast.

Serves 2
handful of small lettuce leaves such as lambs lettuce, watercress or baby spinach
bunch of radishes, halved
bunch of spring onions, roughly chopped
2 hard boiled eggs, quartered
2 large firm tomatoes, quartered
10 anchovy fillets in oil, drained
200g (7 oz) can tuna in oil, drained and flaked
60g (2 oz) black olives
2 tablespoons olive oil
juice of half a lemon
seasoning

1 Arrange the lettuce leaves on 2 plates and top with radishes, spring onions, eggs, tomatoes, anchovies and flakes of tuna. Scatter over the olives and a little seasoning and drizzle with olive oil and lemon juice.

TOMATO AND BASIL SOUP

REALLY EASY!

 This delicious spicy soup can be served hot with
crusty bread for a warming winter supper or
chilled with cheese and crackers for a light
supper in summer.

Serves 2
1 tablespoon olive oil
2 garlic cloves, finely chopped
1 small hot chilli, chopped
300 ml (½ pint) water
2 slices of white bread
400g (14 oz) can chopped tomatoes
few leaves fresh basil, roughly torn
pinch of sugar
seasoning

1 Heat the oil in a large saucepan, add the garlic and
chilli and cook for 5 minutes until softened.

2 Meanwhile, coarsely grate the bread to make crumbs
and add these to the pan with 300 ml (½ pint) of water
and the can of chopped tomatoes. Stir in the sugar and
seasoning, cover and cook for 10 minutes until heated
right through.

3 Stir in the basil leaves, divide into two bowls and serve
with a good sprinkling of black pepper.

SNACKS & STANDBYS

If you feel like a nibble, don't be tempted by crisps or chocolate. Dig deep into your cupboard and see if you can whip up a healthier, more filling snack to keep hunger at bay. However hard you might try, you'll sometimes fancy a bite to eat between meals. It may be because you missed a meal and need something to keep you going or perhaps it's just boredom. Whatever the reason here are a few easy ideas to help you combat a snack attack.

BARBECUED SPARE RIBS

R E A L L Y   E A S Y !

Some supermarkets sell spare ribs cut into small 'mini' ribs. If you can buy them, they are excellent for snack meals.

Serves 2
500g (1 lb) pork spare ribs
2 tablespoons flour

For The Barbecue Sauce
1 tablespoon dark soy sauce
1 tablespoon tomato purée
2 tablespoons clear honey
2 garlic cloves, finely chopped
1 cm (½ inch) piece fresh ginger, peeled and grated
juice of an orange
1 teaspoon English mustard

1 Place the flour, a little seasoning and the ribs together in a plastic bag. Shake the bag to coat the ribs.

2 Mix together all the sauce ingredients. Shake any excess flour off the ribs, dip into the sauce and place on a foil lined grill pan.

3 Place under a hot grill for about 30 minutes, turning and basting frequently with the remaining sauce until brown, shiny and cooked through. In the summer these ribs can be cooked on a barbecue.

GARLIC MUSHROOMS

REALLY EASY!

Serve with warm French bread for a delicious snack or starter.

Serves 1
125g (4 oz) small button mushrooms
30g (1 oz) butter
1 large garlic clove, finely chopped
1 teaspoon lemon juice
1 teaspoon chopped fresh parsley
seasoning

1 Heat the butter until foaming, but not brown. Toss in the mushrooms and garlic and cook for 2 minutes.

2 Add the lemon juice and seasoning, cover with a lid and cook gently for 5 minutes.

3 Remove the lid and cook for a further 5 minutes, until softened. Stir in the parsley and serve.

BARBECUED SPARE RIBS • GARLIC MUSHROOMS

HAMBURGERS

R E A L L Y   E A S Y !

**Home made hamburgers are so quick and cheap
to make that it's really not worth buying them
ready-made, and they freeze well too.**

Serves 2-4
*500g (1 lb) lean minced beef
1 teaspoon Worcestershire sauce
1 small onion, finely chopped
1 tablespoon chopped fresh parsley
seasoning*

1 Place all the ingredients in a bowl and mix well together. Shape the mixture into 4 large, round patties.

2 Pop under a medium grill for around 8 minutes on each side until cooked through. Serve in sesame seed buns with salad and mustard.

POTATO PANCAKES

E A S Y !

These fluffy pancakes can be eaten hot with baked beans or a fried egg for a light lunch or cold as a snack. Try adding different ingredients such as chopped ham, parsley, spring onions, or use Parmesan in place of Cheddar.

Serves 2
500g (1 lb) potatoes, cubed
knob of butter
2 tablespoons milk
60g (2 oz) Cheddar, grated
60g (2 oz) plain flour
seasoning

1 Cook the potatoes in boiling, salted water for 10-15 minutes, until tender.

2 Mash well with the butter, milk and cheese. Stir in the flour and season to taste. Use your hands to shape into about 8 round pancakes about 1 cm (½ inch) thick.

3 Place under a preheated grill and cook gently for about 5 minutes on each side until golden brown. Take care when turning the pancakes over as although they develop a crust on the outside, they are still soft inside.

HAMBURGERS • POTATO PANCAKES

SESAME PRAWN TOASTS

E A S Y !

**If you've ever tried these delicious tit-bits
as a starter in a Chinese restaurant, like me you
probably wondered how they were made.
They are actually really simple to make
yourself, and taste just as good as the
ones that cost a fortune.**

Serves 2
*125g (4 oz) prawns
2.5 cm (1 inch) piece fresh ginger, grated
1 garlic clove, finely chopped
2 teaspoons cornflour
1 egg white
4 slices white bread, crusts removed
2 tablespoons sesame seeds
vegetable oil for frying
seasoning*

1 Finely chop the prawns with a heavy knife and mix together in a bowl with the ginger, garlic and cornflour. Season well.

2 In a separate bowl, whisk the egg white with a fork until frothy. Tip in the prawn mixture and blend well together.

3 Spread evenly onto the bread and cut each slice into 4 fingers or triangles. Sprinkle over the sesame seeds, and press firmly in place.

4 Heat 1 cm (½ inch) of oil in a large frying pan and cook the fingers, prawn-side down first, for 2-3 minutes on each side until crisp and golden. Serve immediately.

POTATO SKINS

REALLY EASY!

Save the flesh scooped out of the potatoes to make another dish such as potato pancakes (page 143), Corned beef hash (page 26) or fish cakes (page 27.).
Americans traditionally serve skins with sour cream but there are lots of ways to eat them – grate over a little cheese, sprinkle with spring onions and pop under the grill to melt the cheese. Or try serving them with a delicious dip such as Guacamole or Tsatziki (pages 146 & 147).

Serves 1
2 potatoes, unpeeled
oil for frying
salt

1 Halve the potatoes lengthwise and boil in lightly salted water for 15 minutes. Drain well and pat dry. Use a spoon to scoop out the potato flesh, leaving a shell about 1 cm (½ inch) thick. Cut each shell into 3 or 4 strips.

2 Heat about 5 cm (2 inches) of vegetable oil in a heavy saucepan and fry the skins for 2-3 minutes until crisp and golden. Sprinkle with a little salt and serve.

SESAME PRAWN TOASTS • POTATO SKINS

GUACAMOLE

**A lovely smooth avocado dip that goes
well with snack crackers, crisps, toasted
French bread or vegetable sticks.**

Serves 1
*1 ripe avocado
juice of half a lemon
1 small garlic clove, finely chopped
1 tablespoon olive oil
a few drops of Tabasco
1 ripe tomato, skinned and diced (optional)
seasoning*

1 Mash all the ingredients well together and season to taste.

TSATZIKI

A fresh tasting dip of cucumber, garlic, mint and yoghurt. Serve with warm pitta bread.

Serves 1

5 cm (2 inch) piece cucumber, coarsely grated
1 garlic clove, finely chopped
1 tablespoon finely chopped onion
150 ml (¼ pint) Greek-style yogurt
1 tablespoon chopped fresh mint
seasoning

1 Mix all the ingredients well together and season to taste. Serve immediately.

FRIED TOASTIES

REALLY EASY!

For those of you who don't have access to a sandwich toaster, a decent non-stick frying pan is all you need to make crispy, golden sandwiches.

Serves 1
knob of butter
2 slices of bread
60g (2 oz) grated cheese
1 tomato, sliced
seasoning

1 Butter the bread and make up a sandwich with the butter on the outside.

2 Heat a non-stick frying pan, Carefully place the sandwich in the pan. Cook for about 3 minutes, pressing down gently with a fish slice until golden brown underneath. Carefully, turn and cook other side. Eat immediately.

TOASTY FILLINGS

Any sort of cheese that melts makes a great toasty filling. Try melting with any of the following:

Wholegrain mustard

Wafer thin ham

Red onion

Spring onions

Chives

Piccalilli

Warm baked beans or spaghetti hoops

Chopped garlic and a couple of torn basil leaves

Olive paste

Mayonnaise

Hot salsa (page 154).

OTHER FILLINGS TO TRY

Scrambled eggs and a little horseradish sauce,

Roasted sweet potato and aubergine salad (page 31)

Diced avocado

Tomato and mayonnaise

Spanish tortilla (page 24),

Macaroni cheese (page 62),

Fried bacon and maple syrup.

MUSHROOM FRITATA

REALLY EASY!

A fritata is a spongy Italian omelette which, like the Spanish tortilla, is cooked slowly, cut into wedges and eaten hot or cold. Left over fritata can be cut into chunks, simmered for a few minutes in a simple tomato sauce and served with buttered new potatoes and salad.

Serves 2
4 eggs, beaten
2 slices of white bread, grated
1 garlic clove, sliced
2 tablespoons chopped fresh parsley
1 tablespoon freshly grated Parmesan
2 tablespoons olive oil
125g (4 oz) mushrooms, sliced
seasoning

1 Mix together the eggs, breadcrumbs, garlic, parsley, and Parmesan and season well.

2 Heat the olive oil in a frying pan and cook the mushrooms for 4-5 minutes until softened. Tip in the egg mixture and smooth over with a spatula.

3 Cook slowly for about 5 minutes, until golden underneath. Carefully turn over and cook the other side until golden.

EGGY BREAD

R E A L L Y E A S Y !

The secret of eggy bread is to leave the bread soaking in the egg for as long as you can, 20 minutes is ideal. One of my most recent concoctions is the eggy bread sandwich, which I've been eating for my breakfast almost every weekend. Simply make up a cheese sandwich, (mozzarella, tomato and basil is my current favourite) and soak and fry in the usual way. If you have any egg mixture left over, pour it on top of the bread as it is cooking in the pan.

Serves 1

1 egg
2 tablespoons milk
2 slices of white bread
vegetable oil for frying
seasoning

1 Beat the egg and milk together in a shallow dish and dip in the bread. Press down with a spatula so the bread absorbs the liquid.

2 Heat a little oil a frying pan and cook the bread for 3-4 minutes on each side until puffed and golden. Drain on kitchen paper and eat straightaway.

SCRAMBLED EGGS ON TOAST

REALLY EASY!

A brilliant snack at any time of the day. Try adding different flavourings or ingredients such as chopped fresh herbs, a spoonful of tartare sauce, chopped ham, or diced tomatoes. Of course if you're celebrating the end of term, the classic addition to scrambled eggs is smoked salmon.

Serves 1
2 eggs
2 tablespoons milk
knob of butter
2 thick slices of hot buttered toast
½ tablespoon freshly grated Parmesan
salt and freshly ground black pepper

1 Lightly beat together the eggs, milk and seasoning.

2 Melt the butter in a small pan. Toss in the eggs and stir with a chopstick or fork until just set, but still a little runny, take care not to over cook.

3 Turn onto the hot toast and sprinkle with a little grated Parmesan and a sprinkling of black pepper.

CORN ON THE COB

REALLY EASY!

V **Make the most of the juicy cobs of corn that are cheap and available in the summer months. You can flavour the butter with herbs, garlic or chilli, if you wish, but I prefer to serve it plain.**

Serves 1
1 corn cob
knob of butter
salt

1 Peel back the husks, remove the silky threads and trim the stem. Bring a large pan of water to the boil, but do not add salt as it hardens the kernels during cooking.

2 Cook in the boiling water for 7 minutes, until the corn is bright yellow. Remove with a slotted spoon, smother with butter and sprinkle with salt. Eat immediately, using your fingers.

SCRAMBLED EGGS ON TOAST • CORN ON THE COB

COURGETTE WHEELS WITH HOT SALSA

EASY!

As a child, whenever I complained of feeling peckish, my mother used to whip up these golden wheels in about 2 minutes.

Serves 2
1 egg
2 tablespoons milk
seasoning
vegetable oil, for frying
2 tablespoons flour
1 large courgette, thinly sliced

For The Salsa
250g (8 oz) ripe tomatoes, finely chopped
2 small chillies, finely chopped
2 garlic cloves, finely chopped
1 small onion, finely chopped
1 tablespoon chopped fresh coriander
1 tablespoon olive oil
seasoning

1 Mix together the tomatoes, chilli, garlic, onion, coriander, olive oil and seasoning and set aside whilst you fry the courgettes.

2 Beat together the egg, milk and a little seasoning. Heat 1 cm (½ inch) of oil in a large frying pan. Season the flour. Dip the courgettes first into the flour, shake of any excess, dip into the egg and then fry for 2 minutes on each side until golden. Drain on kitchen towel and serve immediately with the hot salsa.

WELSH RAREBIT

REALLY EASY!

This method may not be true to the original which is rather time consuming, but it tastes almost as good. Top each slice with a poached egg to make Buck Rarebit.

Serves 1
60g (2 oz) Cheddar, grated
1 teaspoon English mustard
1 tablespoon Worcestershire sauce
small knob of butter
2 slices of toast

1 Beat together the cheese, mustard, Worcestershire sauce and butter to make a paste.

2 Spread on the toast and place under the grill for 3 minutes until bubbling and golden.

SWEETCORN FRITTERS

REALLY EASY!

These crisp little fritters are quickly made from store cupboard ingredients.

Serves 2-3 (Makes about 12)
2 eggs
4 tablespoons milk
90g (3 oz) self-raising flour
½ teaspoon salt
275g (10 oz) can sweetcorn, drained
vegetable oil for frying

1 Beat together the eggs, milk, self raising flour and salt until smooth. Stir in the sweetcorn.

2 Heat 1 cm (½ inch) vegetable oil in a large frying pan and carefully drop in large spoonfuls of the mixture. Cook for 3-4 minutes on each side until crisp and golden. Serve with mayonnaise or make a quick topping by stirring some chopped chives into Greek yogurt.

BUFFALO CHICKEN WINGS

REALLY EASY!

Chicken wings baked with a spicy, devilled sauce. You won't be able to eat these without licking your fingers.

Serves 2
1 small onion, very finely chopped
2 garlic cloves, crushed
1 tablespoon clear honey
2 tablespoons vegetable oil
3 tablespoons tomato ketchup
2 tablespoons Worcestershire sauce
few drops of Tabasco
12 chicken wings

1 Preheat the oven to 200C,400F,Gas 6. Place the onion, garlic, honey, vegetable oil, tomato ketchup, Worcestershire sauce and Tabasco together in a small saucepan. Simmer together for 5 minutes.

2 Place the chicken wings on a baking sheet and brush all over with the sauce. Bake for about 30 minutes, basting occasionally with sauce, until cooked through and golden brown.

SWEETCORN FRITTERS • BUFFALO CHICKEN WINGS

SPINACH FRITTERS

REALLY EASY!

 This is a Spanish tapas dish that you can eat just as a snack or as an accompaniment to grilled meat or fish or with rice as part of a vegetarian meal.

Serves 2

1 egg
½ teaspoon chilli powder
pinch nutmeg
2 tablespoons freshly grated Parmesan
350g (12 oz) spinach, cooked if fresh or thawed if frozen, squeezed dry
45g (1½ oz) fresh breadcrumbs
seasoning
olive oil, for frying

1 Beat together the egg, chilli, nutmeg, Parmesan and seasoning. Mix with the spinach and breadcrumbs and shape into 4 round patties.

2 Heat a little oil in a frying pan and cook the fritters for 3 - 4 minutes on each side until crisp and golden.

INDEX